CW01596938

Level 1 Certificate for IT Users
for City & Guilds

Using the Internet

for Office XP

Level 1

Tina Lawton

Endorsed by City & Guilds

www.heinemann.co.uk
✓ Free online support
✓ Useful weblinks
✓ 24 hour online ordering

01865 888058

Heinemann
Inspiring generations

Heinemann Educational Publishers
Halley Court, Jordan Hill, Oxford, OX2 8EJ
A division of Harcourt Education Ltd

Heinemann is a registered trademark of Harcourt Education Ltd

OXFORD MELBOURNE AUCKLAND
JOHANNESBURG BLANTYRE GABORNE
IBADAN PORTSMOUTH NH(USA) CHICAGO

First published in 2004
2007 2006 2005 2004
10 9 8 7 6 5 4 3 2 1

A catalogue record for this book is available from the British Library on request.

ISBN 0 435 46273 3

Acknowledgements
The authors and publishers would like to thank the following for permission to reproduce screenshots: Microsoft (throughout book); Figure 1.7 Virgin Net; Figure 1.8c Museum of Antiquities of the University and Society of Antiquaries of Newcastle upon Tyne; Figure 1.9b 5 Star Network Ltd; 2.3 blueyonder.co.uk; page 46 Realplayer, part of RealNetworks; Figures 3.20–23 AltaVista Internet Operations Ltd; Figure 3.24 Ask Jeeves; Figure 5.1 Symantec; Figure 5.6 ©1999–2004 Zone Labs, Inc., 475 Brannan Street, Suite 300, San Francisco, CA 94107 USA. All rights reserved.

The publishers have made every effort to trace the copyright holders, but if they have inadvertently overlooked any, they will be pleased to make the necessary arrangements at the first opportunity.

Typeset by Techset Ltd, Gateshead
Printed and bound in Great Britain by Thomson Litho Ltd, Glasgow

Websites
Please note that the examples of websites suggested in this book were up to date at the time of writing. It is essential for tutors to review each site before using it to ensure that the URL is still accurate and the content is appropriate. We suggest that tutors bookmark useful sites and consider enabling students to access them through the school or college intranet.

Contents

Introduction

City & Guilds e-Quals is an exciting new range of IT qualifications developed with leading industry experts. These comprehensive, progressive awards cover everything from getting to grips with basic IT to gaining the latest professional skills.

The range consists of both user and practitioner qualifications. User qualifications (Levels 1–3) are ideal for those who use IT as part of their job or in life generally, while Practitioner qualifications (Levels 2–3) have been developed for those who need to boost their professional skills in, for example, networking or software development.

e-Quals boasts on-line testing and a dedicated website with news and support materials and web-based training. The qualifications reflect industry standards and meet the requirements of the National Qualifications Framework.

With e-Quals you will not only develop your expertise, you will gain a qualification that is recognised by employers all over the world.

This unit is about the Internet – a global source of information, ideas, commerce and communication. From the first steps back in the 1960s to the Internet we access today, there have been many changes, but perhaps the most startling is the way we can access all these services from the comfort of our own home.

It is often said that you can find anything and everything on the Net. While this is probably a little short of the truth, there is undoubtedly a wealth of exciting and interesting things to discover and explore. Once you start to surf the Net it's easy to forget the time, the only reminder is the phone bill when it eventually arrives! Working through the sections, you will be able to learn about a wide range of topics from browsers to broadband, surfing to service providers, and modems to messages. You will be able to find out how to keep in touch and keep your computer safe.

Throughout the unit there are challenges to test your knowledge and opportunities to 'try it out' for yourself. At the end of the book there are assignments for you to use as practice to make sure you're absolutely ready to pass the real thing.

Although this book covers the syllabus for the City & Guilds IT Users Level 1 Certificate Unit 005, it would be just as helpful for anyone wanting to learn how to 'surf' the Net.

Acknowledgements

My grateful thanks to: Stuart for his constant support and understanding – not to mention the endless cups of tea; Keith and Anna for their advice when I got stuck; everyone who has contributed to the development of the Internet – I used it frequently to research this book!; and last, but not least, Pen, for believing I could do it.

Section 1 Getting started

You will learn to

- Identify the equipment required to use the Internet
- Identify factors that determine Internet speed
- Identify the elements that comprise a URL
- Describe terminology associated with the Internet
- Identify typical services available via the Internet
- Identify the advantages and disadvantages of using the Internet
- Identify various ways in which a computer virus may be distributed across the Internet

Introduction: A global network

When two computers are linked together to share information and resources, they form a network. The Internet is a global network, which links millions of computers and smaller networks in many countries across the world. Using the Internet, it is as easy to communicate with someone in Australia as it is to send a message to your work colleague at the next workstation.

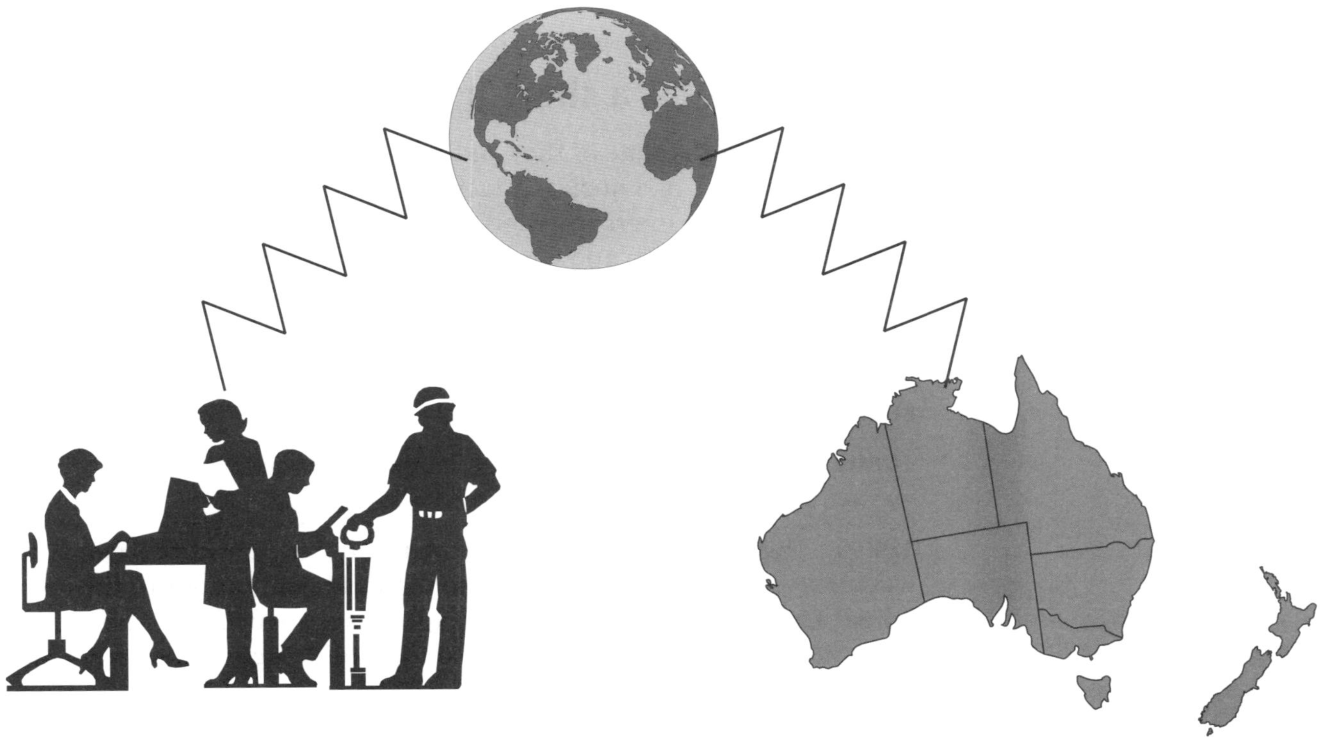

Figure 1.1 The Internet enables people throughout the world to communicate with one another by computer

Some of the computers on the Internet which store, sort and distribute information are called 'hosts' or servers, others, like your computer at home or work, are called 'clients'. Whatever type of computer, server or client, they can only talk to each other if they are connected by cables, radio waves or satellite. Usually your home or work computer will be connected to the Internet using the telephone lines.

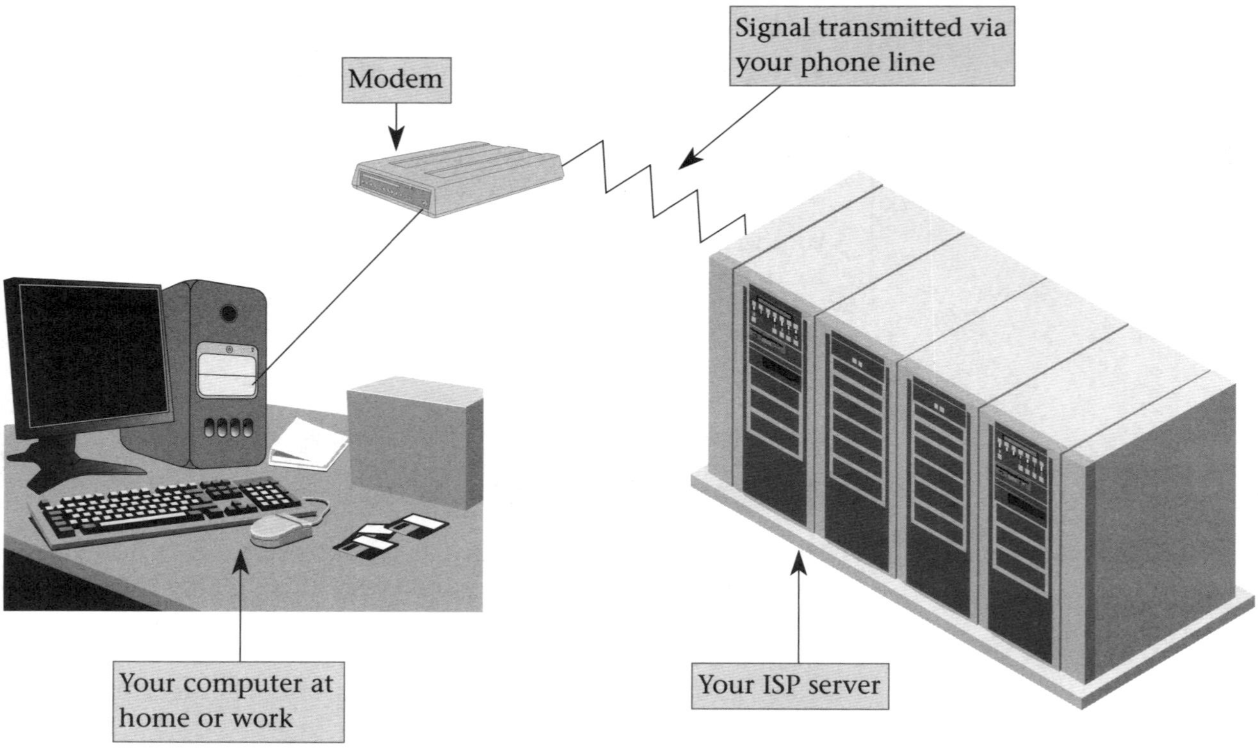

Figure 1.2 How your computer is connected to the Internet

The Internet – a short history

1960s During the time of the Cold War, the US Defence Department, worried over fears of a nuclear attack, began a project to link computers over America in a giant interconnected network. If part of the network was destroyed, information and communication could be re-routed through the remaining computers. This network was called ARPANET (Advanced Research Projects Agency NETwork).

1970s Supercomputers in universities and companies across America became linked into the network to share research information.

1980s A network called NSFNET (National Science Foundation NETwork) was set up to exchange non-commercial information.

1990s This was a period of rapid expansion of the network when access was opened up to everyone, from commercial organisations to the user at home. The development of the millions of pages which make up the World Wide Web made the Internet easier to use and brought information, data and e-commerce to people across the world.

World Wide Web

The Internet and the **World Wide Web** (or Web as it is usually called) are terms which are used interchangeably, but they are not the same. The Internet is the underlying structure of connected computers, whereas the Web is a software application that sits on top of the communication hardware and software that is the Internet. It is made up of millions of **web pages**, which have been uploaded to a host server so that you can view them with special software called a **browser**. Web pages are written in a special text-based language called **HTML (HyperText Markup Language)**.

Equipment for connecting to the Internet

The Internet is a global network, which links millions of computers in many countries of the world. You, at home or work, can link into this network by using your **telephone line**, or **cable** connection.

Getting connected requires certain hardware and software. First you'll need a **computer**, but it doesn't need to have the latest and fastest processor to be able to access all the vast amounts of information on the Net, although it does help to have plenty of RAM (Random Access Memory) to process the graphics which invariably come with web pages. If you have a multimedia computer you will have **speakers** and a **sound card** inside the processing unit, so that you can hear sounds on web pages or listen to music from radio stations across the world. If you plan to use broadband technologies to connect to the Net you may need a more modern computer equipped with a USB (Universal Serial Bus) port.

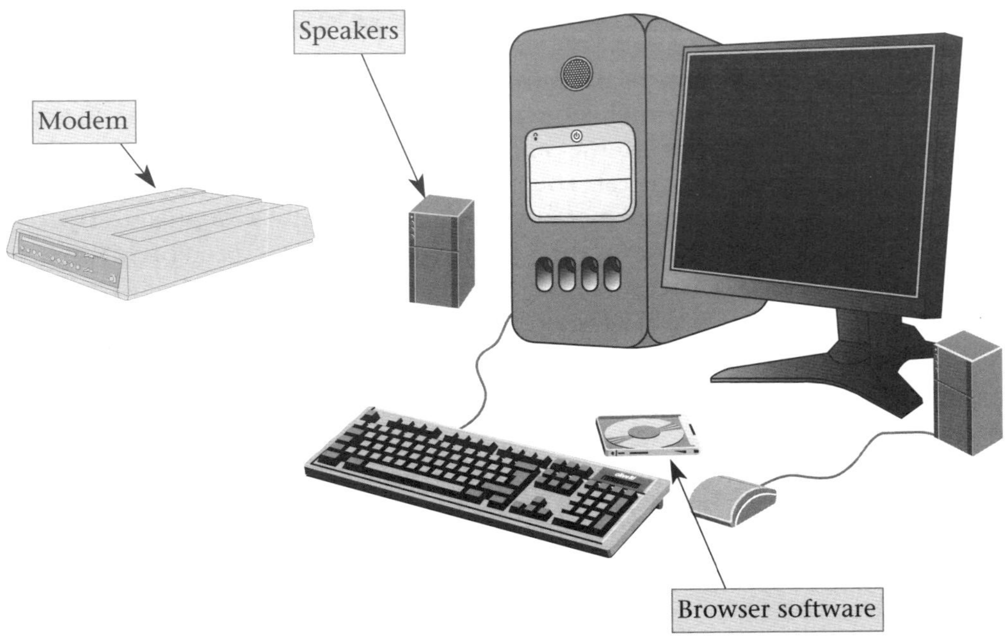

Figure 1.3 The hardware and software you need for accessing the Internet

From your home computer you will need a **modem** to connect to your phone line. Your PC processes **digital** data, represented as either a 0 or a 1 (binary), by turning on or off a series of switches. Your telephone system is an **analogue** device which transmits signals in a continuous wave. A modem is a device which translates analogue signals into digital data and vice versa, and is called this because it **mo**dulates and **dem**odulates the signal so the telephone system and the computer can understand each other.

Modems can be external or internal, but in either case they need to be connected to both your telephone line and your computer. For broadband connections, modern technologies allow the modem to be connected to your computer via wireless signals, so you won't have cables to connect, making for a tidier workplace. To access the Internet you will need an **ISP** (**Internet Service Provider**) to act as your 'gateway' to the Internet.

The final piece of the jigsaw is the **software** – called a **browser**. This is a program that translates the information on the Net into documents you can see on screen. Most browsers have other useful functions too, like access to e-mail, downloading files, saving web pages and allowing you to print out information. The browsers most people are familiar with are **Internet Explorer** and **Netscape**. Most of the instructions and illustrations in this book will use Internet Explorer, but many of the functions are common to both browsers.

There are also many other smaller software programs which will make surfing the Net more enjoyable – these are called **plug-ins**. They will enable you to watch video clips, hear music and watch animations.

Try it out!

Find out which browser you have installed on your machine.

How fast can you go?

One of the most essential pieces of hardware you need to connect to the Internet is the modem. As the modem handles the transfer of data between the Internet and your computer, the speed at which it can transmit that data is critical. This speed is measured in **bits per second** (a bit is the smallest unit of memory or storage), usually shortened to **bps**. Most new computers these days will have modems with a speed of **56Kbps** (Kilobits per second). Anything much slower than this, and you may find yourself waiting for web pages to download onto your screen, which can be frustrating.

Any connection to the Internet using your normal phone line will be limited to 56Kbps. The speed of data transmission will also be decided by the **bandwidth** of the communication lines being used to make the connection. Some of the newer technologies, such as ISDN (Integrated Services Digital Technology) and broadband, can transfer data at a faster rate. Broadband connections can download data at speeds of up to 512 Kbps, and, as technology develops, download speeds are getting faster all the time.

There is another factor, apart from modem speed and bandwidth, that can affect the rate of data transfer. Just like the main roads at rush hour, the Internet, which is often referred to as the Information Superhighway, can become a crawl as thousands of users log on at peak times. It's always worth checking the time if things seem to be very slow – it may just be because businesses in America have suddenly connected to the Net at the start of their working day! Your modem software will usually tell you the speed of your connection when you are online. You can access this dialogue box by double clicking on the connected icon on the taskbar.

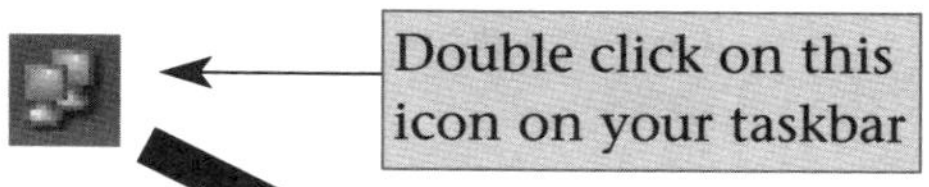

Figure 1.4 Connection icon

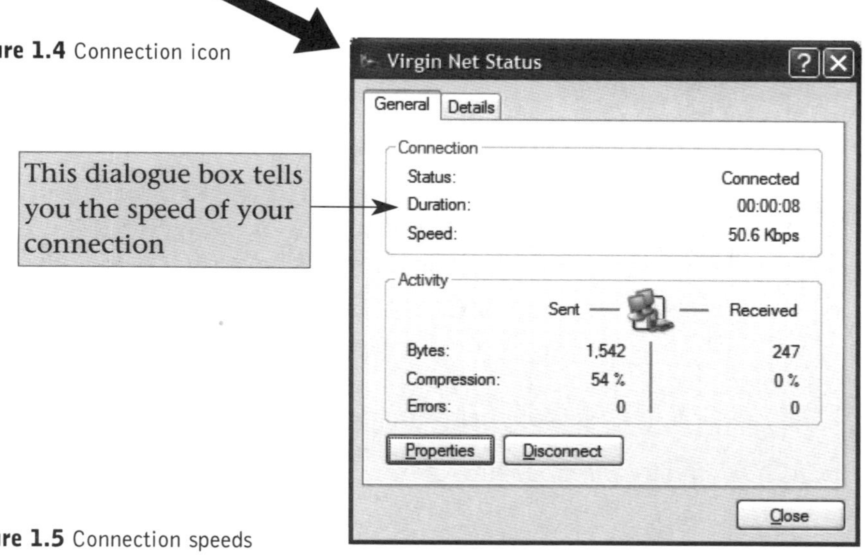

Figure 1.5 Connection speeds

If there are lots of people using the server you are connected to, or if everyone is trying to connect to your ISP, then this too can slow down the speed you can transfer data.

Not surprisingly, if you are downloading big files or lots of graphics, it can seem to take forever. Your modem might be working at peak efficiency, but you need to remember that the bigger the file/graphic, the longer it will take to appear on your screen.

Information: Finding the right address

With so many millions of computers forming the Internet, it is essential that each computer knows where it is and where all the other computers are. This is done by means of unique addresses, called **Internet Protocol (IP)** addresses. IP addresses are usually in the form of a series of numbers which would be difficult to remember, so each computer is given a name too – this is the **domain name**. This is usually in three parts and gives details about where the computer is located. This is an example of a domain name:

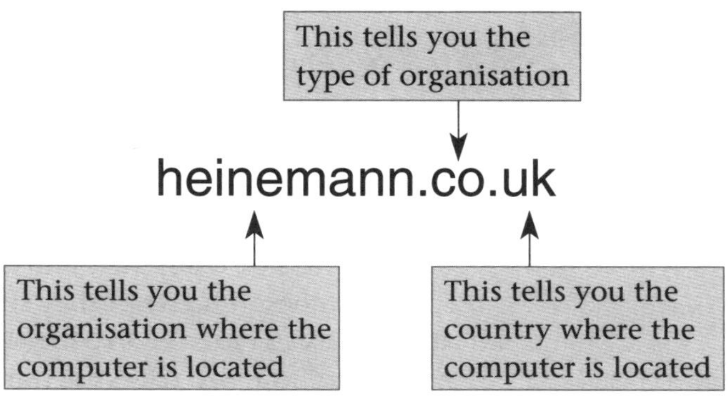

Remember:

When using Internet addresses, it is important to get the address absolutely spot on. All the full stops (usually called 'dots') must be used and there mustn't be any spaces between any characters. The address shown in the example would be spoken as: Heinemann dot co dot uk.

Some of the codes for organisations are:

ac	an academic organisation
co or **com**	a commercial organisation
edu	an educational institution
gov	a government body
net	an organisation involved in running the Net
org	a non-profit-making organisation

As the Internet gets bigger and more computers join, the list of organisation codes will grow.

America doesn't have a country code tagged on after the last full stop; which would be one way to tell if it's an American address. But most other countries have their own code, such as:

au	Australia	**ca**	Canada
de	Germany	**nl**	Netherlands
fr	France	**uk**	United Kingdom

The 'co.uk' part of the address is referred to as the **top level domain**.

URLs (Uniform Resource Locators)

Not all computers and networks talk the same language, so a universal set of rules was created so that all computers could understand each other. This set of rules is called **TCP/IP (Transmission Control Protocol/Internet Protocol)**.

Using TCP will make sure that when data is sent from one computer to another it arrives at its destination safely. If a picture was being sent across the Net it would be broken down into little packets of data. Each packet would contain information about where it had come from and where it was going to – like an address label. When the packets reach their destination, the computer reassembles them into the original image. If the packets didn't have their own address tags, they could get lost along the way!

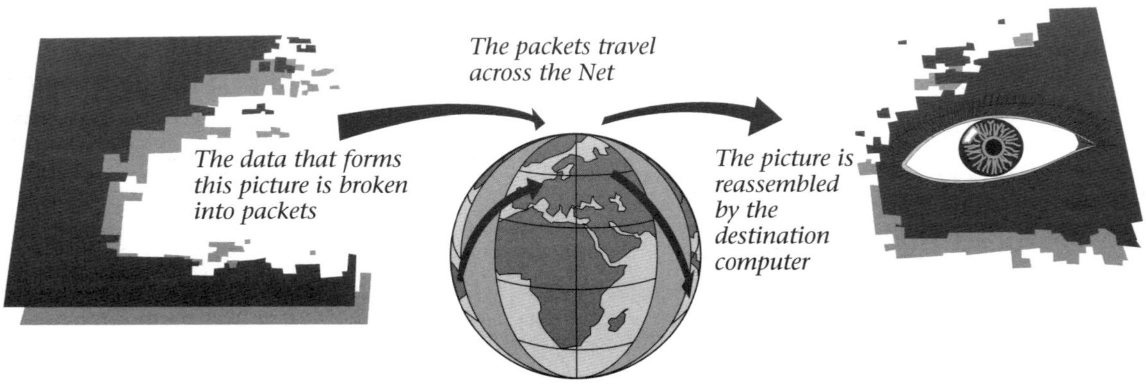

Figure 1.6 How TCP/IP is used to transfer data across the Net

On the Internet, computers and networks also use protocols to communicate, so that it doesn't matter if they speak different languages. This is known as **HyperText Transfer Protocol (HTTP)**. This is the standard set of rules governing how web pages are transferred over the Internet.

A **Uniform Resource Locator (URL)** is the Internet address of a particular web page. These addresses begin with **http://** followed by **www** to indicate that it's a page on the Web.

Web addresses will look something like this example:

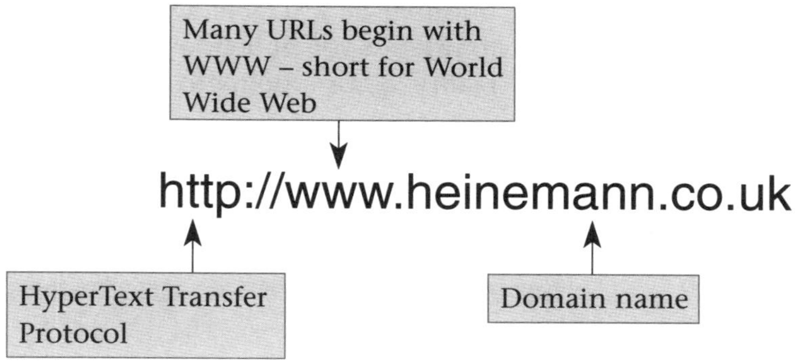

Remember:

Don't forget to type any web addresses exactly as they are written – no spaces and watch the dots!

If you want to download software from a web site, such as a newer version of your browser program, you would use **File Transfer Protocol (FTP)**. This is yet another set of protocols which are needed to copy files over the Net. The files are stored on servers all over the world, called FTP sites. Associated with FTP is **Telnet**, which is a service that allows users to connect to a remote ISP and use it as their own. This service requires FTP to transfer users' files to the remote system. This system is often used in libraries.

Try it out!

Find a list of 10 common URLs from television, magazines, books, radio, adverts, etc. One very common one is: www.bbc.co.uk

Homepage

Many web sites are made up of several web pages linked together. Just like the book you read needs a cover to tell you a little about what's inside, so the web site needs a **homepage.** This is the introductory page that tells you what information the site contains.

The address of the homepage will use the main URL, with a little extra information added to tell the computer exactly where the page is. It may look something like this:

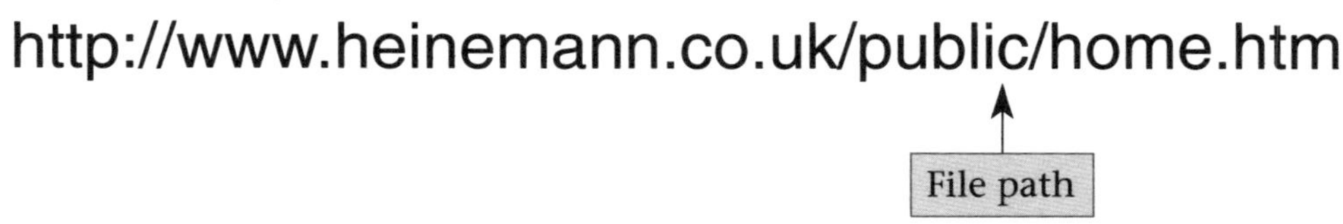

The 'public/home.htm' part of the address is called the **file path** and tells the computer which file the page is stored in and the name of the directory where the file can be found.

What's on the Internet?

Many people would answer this question by saying almost everything or anything. This is not exactly true, however, there is certainly a great deal of information available. Once connected to the Net you can find something to interest you and enjoy, from music to messages, research to virtual reality, and shopping to share buying.

The following are some of the many things you might want to discover.

Communication

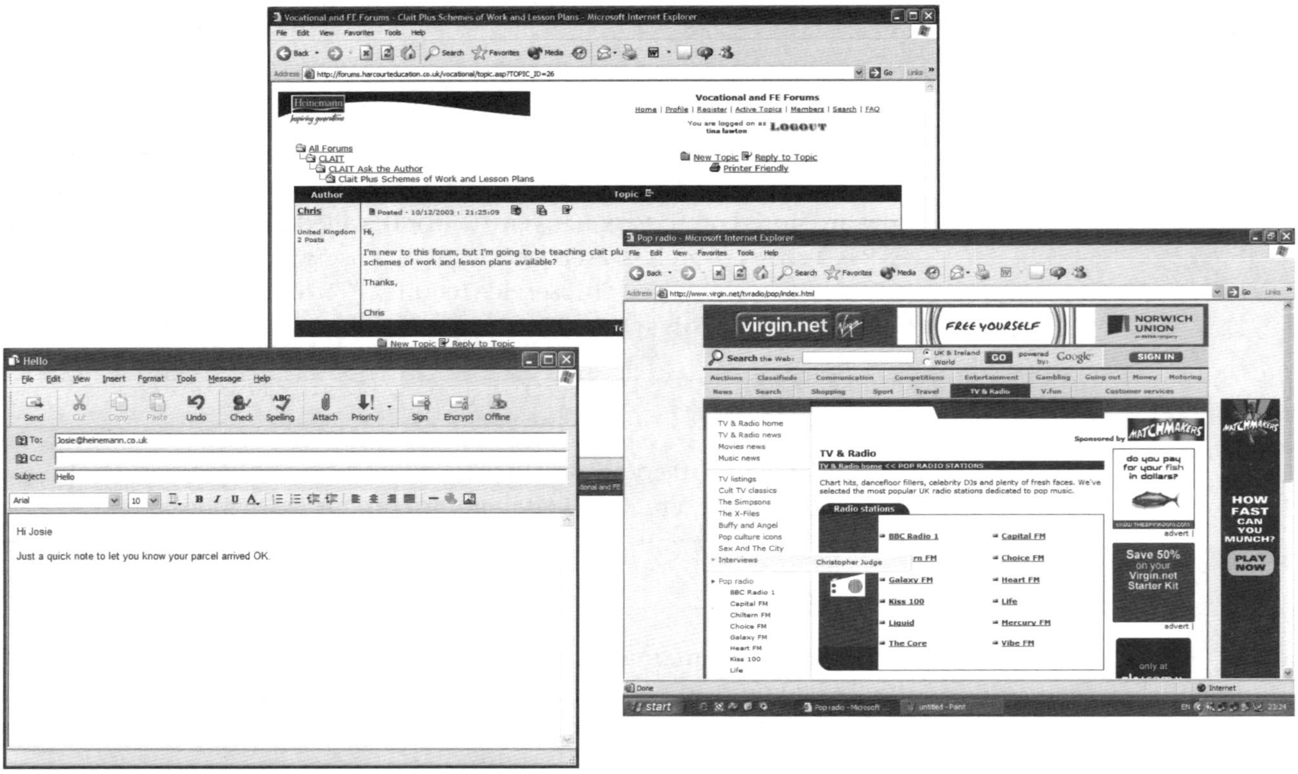

Figure 1.7 Examples of what you get on the Internet

You can send **electronic mail**, usually called **e-mail**, to friends, family and work colleagues across the world. This rapid communication can be cheaper and much quicker than the traditional postal system, often referred to as 'snail mail'.

Using **Internet phones** you can chat to friends in Australia for just the price of a local call. Add a web camera (**web cam**) and they can watch as you talk!

You can '**chat**' online, but using text instead of talk. Special programs will tell you if your friends are also online and ready to exchange gossip or their latest news.

If discussion is your thing, you can join **newsgroups**, where you can exchange views with other like-minded people on just about anything. Be careful, though, your contributions are there for everyone to read – it's not a private conversation!

If you want to discuss important business matters with colleagues in different offices over the country, or even abroad, you could use **video**

conferencing to save time and money. Using a network link, computer, video camera, microphone and speakers, you can hold a meeting without leaving the comfort of your home or office.

You can listen in to music or news on **Internet radio** and keep in touch with what is happening or what are the latest best selling records in the current charts from countries as far afield as America and Australia.

Information

From the millions of files on the Net, you can find out anything from how to complete the project you've been given for coursework or what your Stars have got in store for you. This information can be in many forms, which could include text, pictures, video clips, music and sounds. **Researching information** is probably one of the most well known and well used facilities the Net has to offer.

From the comfort of your own home you can take a **virtual tour** of many famous buildings, art galleries, museums, monuments, almost anywhere. Some virtual tours can recreate the way people lived in the past or give you a taste of the future. From the White House in America to the huts of the Stone Age, you can go round some of the wonders of the world.

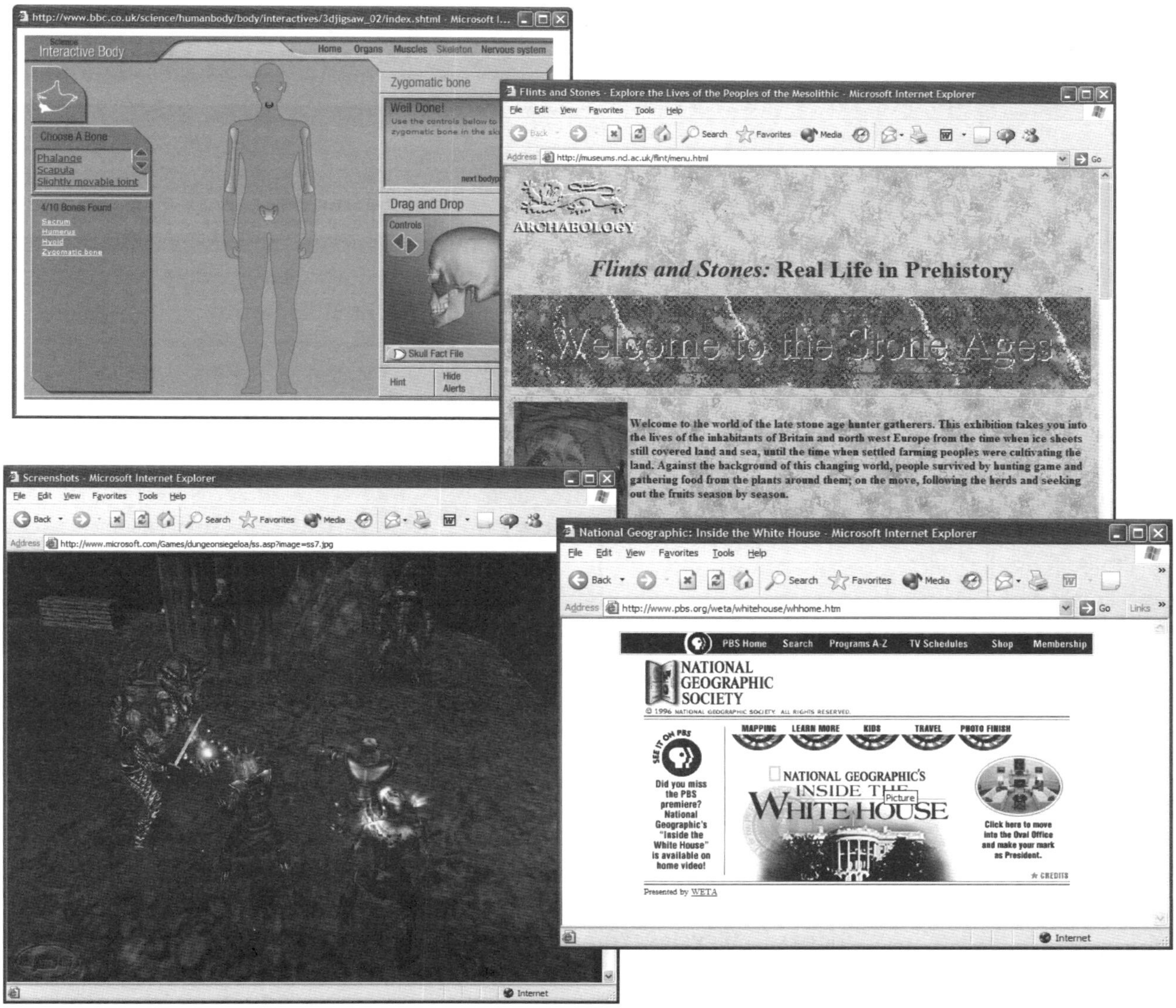

Figure 1.8 Some of the things that you can find on the Internet

Programs

The Internet can provide access to software programs that you can copy to your own computer. This is called **downloading**.

Some of the programs are free for you to use **(Freeware)**, others you may need to pay for, although you can often try them out for a short while to see if you like them (e.g. **Shareware** or **Trialware)**.

Quite often, **updates** or **bug fixes** can be downloaded from the Internet. Updates are files or small programs which will improve some of the functions of your applications. Sometimes new software is released but, even after many trials, there may still be small glitches in the program. These are often called **bugs**. When the company who wrote the software is told, they can release files or a code which will fix the bugs and stop the problem happening.

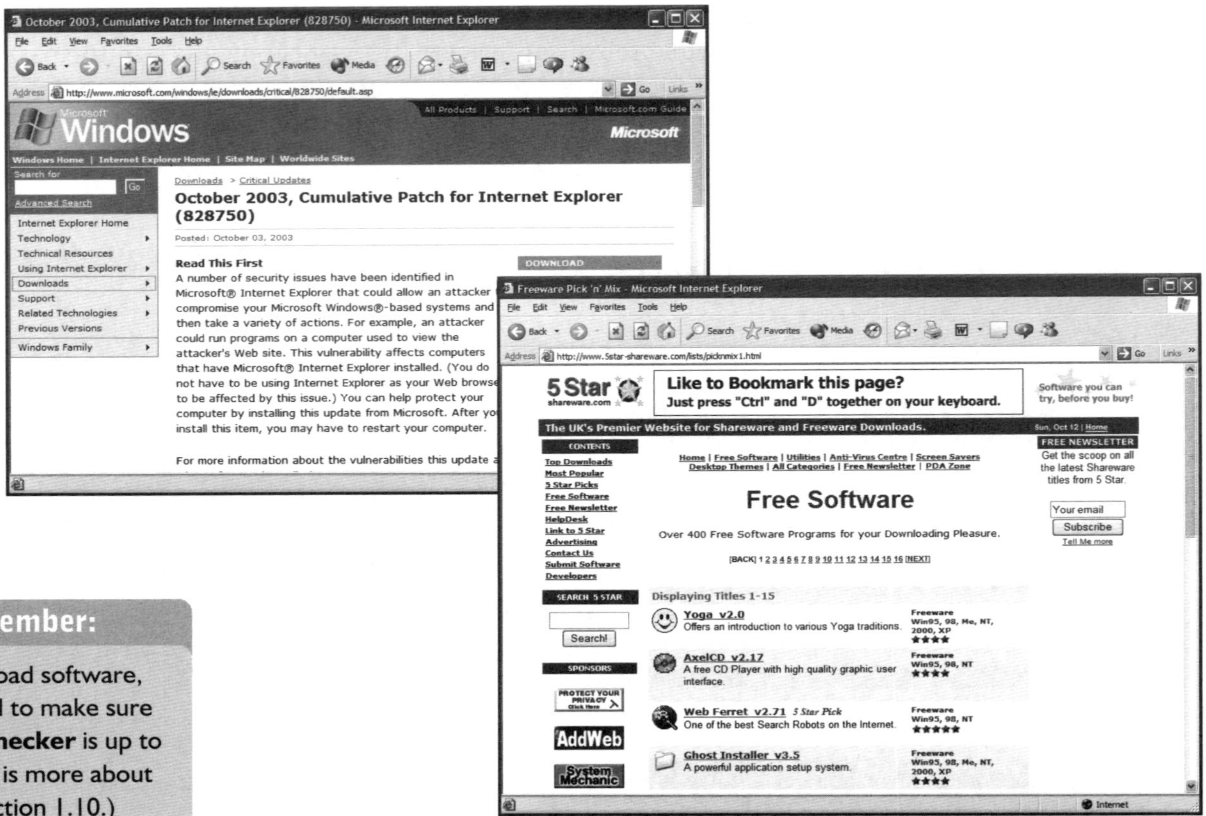

Remember:

If you download software, you will need to make sure your **virus checker** is up to date. (There is more about viruses in Section 1.10.)

Figure 1.9 Examples of free software

Other programs will let you play games, listen to music and read documents produced in a special format.

Services

There is a wide range of **services** available on the Net. You can buy almost anything online, from flowers to footwear, music to motor vehicles, or books to bicycles. You can book tickets for your holiday, seek out a weather forecast to see if you need to pack your umbrella, and check your bank balance afterwards! This is called **e-commerce (electronic commerce)** – a way of doing business online.

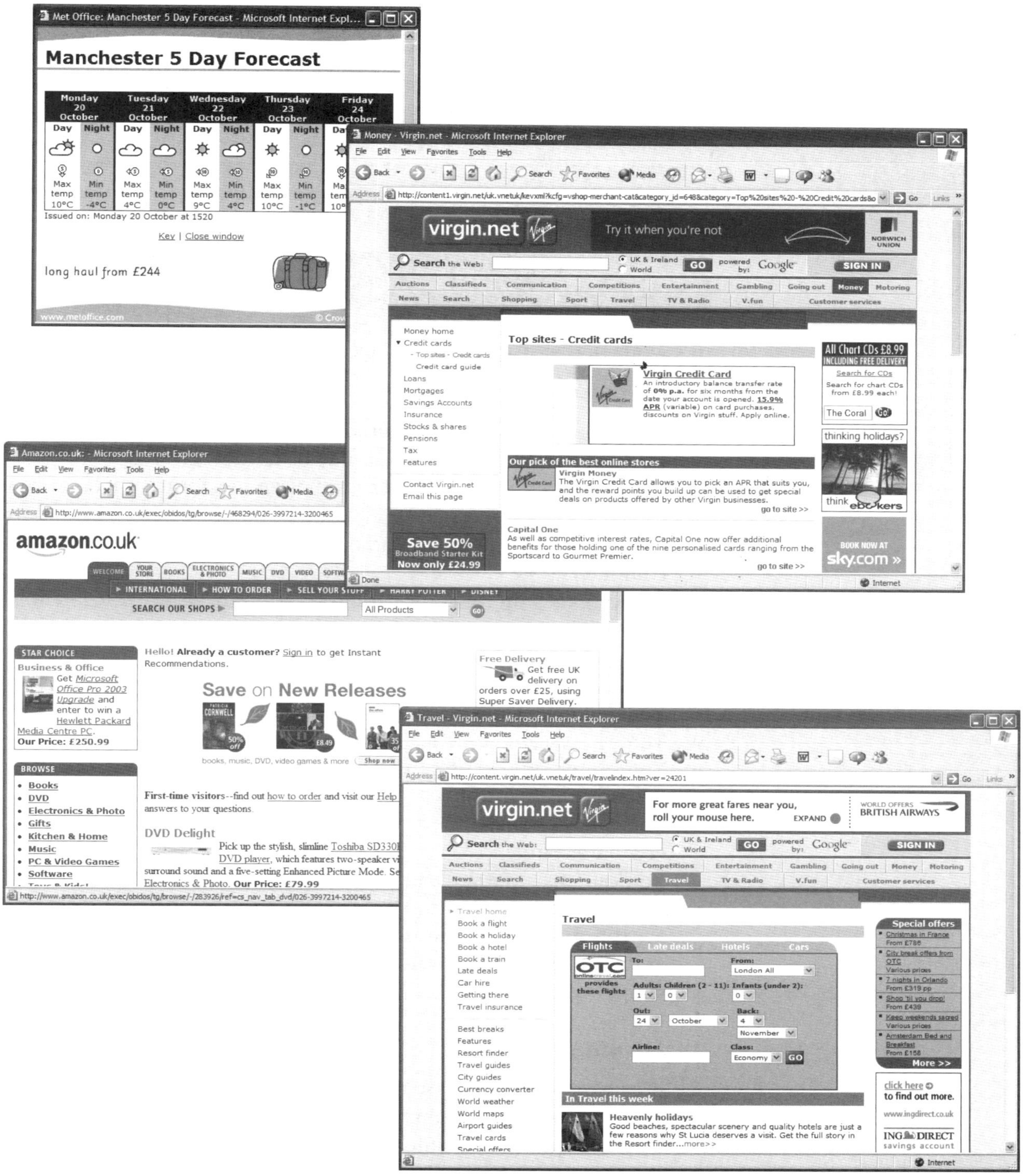

Figure 1.10 Examples of services you can find on the Web

Many companies will advertise on the Web, and provide links to their lists of items for sale so that you can quickly find what you want. You can pay for your goods electronically, by entering your credit or debit card details. The pages where you would enter such sensitive information usually have special security features so that your information can't be misused.

Try it out!

Ask your family and friends if they have ever bought something over the Internet, such as books, music, etc. What did they think about the service? Does it seem a popular thing to do?

Pros and cons

It's worth looking at the advantages and disadvantages of the Internet.

Advantages

- With e-mail you can communicate with other people halfway across the world almost instantly (and it may be cheaper).
- Communication via the Internet is often less formal than conventional methods.
- You can send copies of documents, pictures, music clips, etc. to another computer.
- You can keep up to date with information, news, weather – almost anything, in fact.
- You can play games, either on your own or across a link with other players as far afield as China, Russia, or even the Arctic!
- You can review new software before buying it.
- You can research practically any topic you can think of.
- You can download files, updates and bug fixes to make your computer work more effectively.
- You can seek advice on a whole range of things, from an illness to a computer virus.
- You can chat to friends in any corner of the world.
- You can go shopping online, check your bank balance, buy the tickets for the theatre and the train to get there – the list of services is endless. This is very useful if you live in the countryside far from shopping centres.

Disadvantages

- Because of the more casual approach to business, people could forget that an agreement by e-mail is legally binding.
- Masses of junk mail could end up in your Inbox – just like it does through your letterbox!
- There are always security issues, especially if you are buying goods over the Internet.
- People can get addicted to using the Internet and spend many hours at their computer. This could be expensive in call charges, and could be a health and safety issue.
- There is a great deal of concern about some of the unsuitable material on the Internet, such as pornographic material. This is especially worrying when children have access to the Internet.
- No-one controls the Internet, which certainly allows users a great deal of freedom of speech and access, but this lack of control means it is open to misuse and exploitation.

- In a technological society where information is power, people who don't have access to this information can be at a disadvantage in work and education.
- Developing countries may not have the money to invest in technology and could be disadvantaged by not having access to all the information and services available on the Internet.

Try it out!

This is not an exhaustive list of the advantages and disadvantages of the Internet. Ask your friends and colleagues what they think and see if you can add your own ideas.

Beware of viruses!

A **virus** is a small piece of code deliberately buried inside a program to cause mischief. When the program is run, the virus starts running too. Some viruses are written as a joke to display a message on your screen or make your computer beep every now and then, but others can do a lot of damage to the data in your files and even erase all the information on your hard drive. There are thousands of different viruses and new ones are being invented all the time. The software which can find and clean out a virus is called **anti-virus** software.

Viruses can be distributed across the Internet in several ways:

- Software downloaded from the Internet may have a virus. This could be from software which has been illegally copied (usually called pirated software) or shareware which has been infected. The malicious code would be buried in an **executable** program (the programs which run applications – i.e. execute them) so that running the program releases the virus – a bit like sneezing!
- Viruses can be transmitted by an **e-mail attachment**. A plain text e-mail is harmless, but a file sent with the e-mail as an attachment could carry a virus. You should always be suspicious of an e-mail attachment from someone you don't know, but if your friend's computer is infected, they might send you an attachment which hides a virus without realising it.
- A **macro virus** is a type of computer virus that's hidden inside a macro in a document, template, or add-in. A macro is a recorded set of actions which can be replayed to save time, such as changing fonts in Word (you can assign a 'hotkey' to a macro, similar to Ctrl + V to paste into a document). Any documents with a macro virus that you download from the Internet can infect your computer and, if you send the document to others, it can infect their computers too.
- **Hackers** are people who break into other people's computer systems and open files. They can insert a virus into these files and cause havoc to the system. If you happened to download one of these files, you too may find the virus on your computer.

The only safeguard against infecting your machine is to use an anti-virus utility which you should **update** and **use** regularly. Run your virus checker to scan any files you download or receive *before* you open them, to be on the safe side.

Try it out!

Can you find any information, in newspapers or computer journals, about a recent virus scare? What effect did it have?

→ Check your knowledge

1 How are the Internet and the World Wide Web different?

2 What hardware and software do you need to connect to the Internet?

3 Give a brief description of the following:

- **a** HTML
- **b** ISP
- **c** FTP
- **d** Browser
- **e** URL
- **f** HTTP

4 What are the possible reasons for a slow Internet connection?

5 What information is contained in the domain name?

6 Identify the parts of the following URL:
http://www.usingit.co.uk/homepage.htm

7 List and describe four ways of communicating over the Internet.

8 What is e-commerce?

9 List *five* advantages and *five* disadvantages of using the Internet.

10 Describe the ways viruses can be transmitted across the Internet.

Section 2 Getting connected

You will learn to

- Sign up to an Online Service
- Select an ISP
- Describe the main points to take into consideration when choosing an Internet Service Provider (ISP)
  - ☐ Subscription fee
  - ☐ Special deals, e.g. free provision and types of support
  - ☐ Local access number
  - ☐ Speed of connection
- Identify the steps in subscribing to an ISP
- Identify the steps in signing up to connection software
- Install browser software
- Load browser software
- Use a modem/leased line to connect to the Internet

Online Services and Internet Service Providers

To get connected to the Internet, you have to first decide whether to go for an **Online Service** or an **Internet Service Provider (ISP)**. Either will provide you with a gateway to the Internet, but before you make your decision about which one to choose, it's worth spending some time finding out a little more about what they each offer and which one suits your needs best.

Online Service

There is only one major provider of Online Services – **AOL (America Online)**. The software for this service is provided free on CD-ROM. All you do is load the software by following the onscreen instructions, enter your debit or credit card number, and then you are ready to go.

It is important not to confuse Online Services with the Internet itself. As an Online Service member you will have access to a range of member-only facilities, such as discussion forums, information and shopping, as well as the Internet. Online Services tend to have good built-in help facilities, the members-only content should be safe and has an easy-to-use interface.

Online Services charge a fixed monthly fee, and on top of that there is the cost of phone calls. You might also find that outside the 'clubhouse' of the members-only area, the information doesn't travel quite as quickly as it does in a direct connection to the Internet.

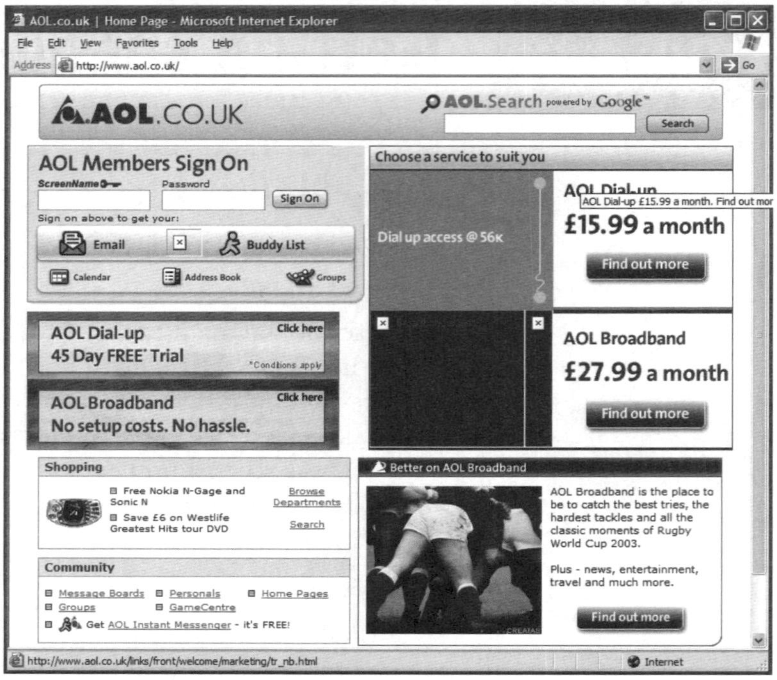

Figure 2.1 AOL provides Online Services

Internet Service Providers

An Internet Service Provider provides access to the Internet. There are many ISPs, and the choice can be bewildering for a newcomer to the Net. Essentially they are very similar, mainly using Internet Explorer or Netscape as their browser, but they will have different logos on the start-up screens, and may have different icons on your desktop.

An ISP runs a network that connects to other parts of the Internet. It has a bank of modems that you can call from your PC at home or work. The services your ISP provides doesn't just stop at Internet access, they can provide other important functions such as the following:

- Storing messages sent to you until you collect them next time you log on.
- Providing web space for you to upload your own information and web pages so that other people can access your site whether your computer is switched on or not.
- Providing other areas for subscribers to use, such as online magazines, chat rooms, information services.
- Multiple e-mail addresses, so that everyone in the family can have their own e-mail facilities.
- Providing help facilities if something goes wrong.

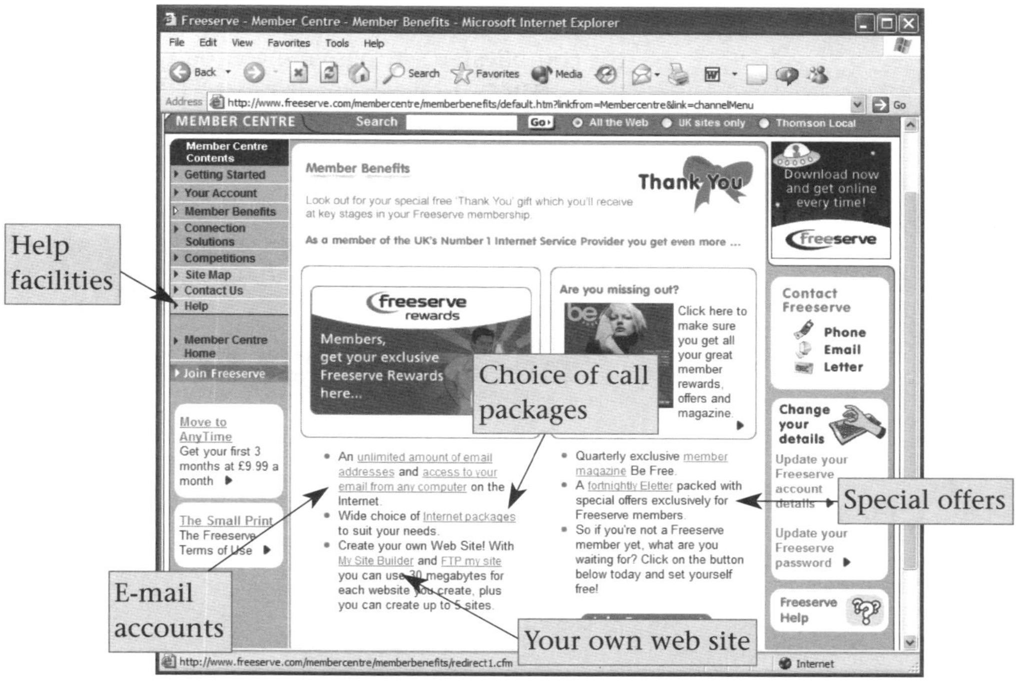

Figure 2.2 An ISP provides a range of services

Not all ISPs provide all these services, but many do. Your choice of ISP will depend on which of these services you might want.

Most ISPs now offer their services free, i.e. you don't pay a monthly subscription charge, but you do pay for phone calls. Some ISPs offer packages to make surfing cheaper, for example by giving free Internet calls during the evenings and weekends for a small monthly fee, or other similar premium rate services.

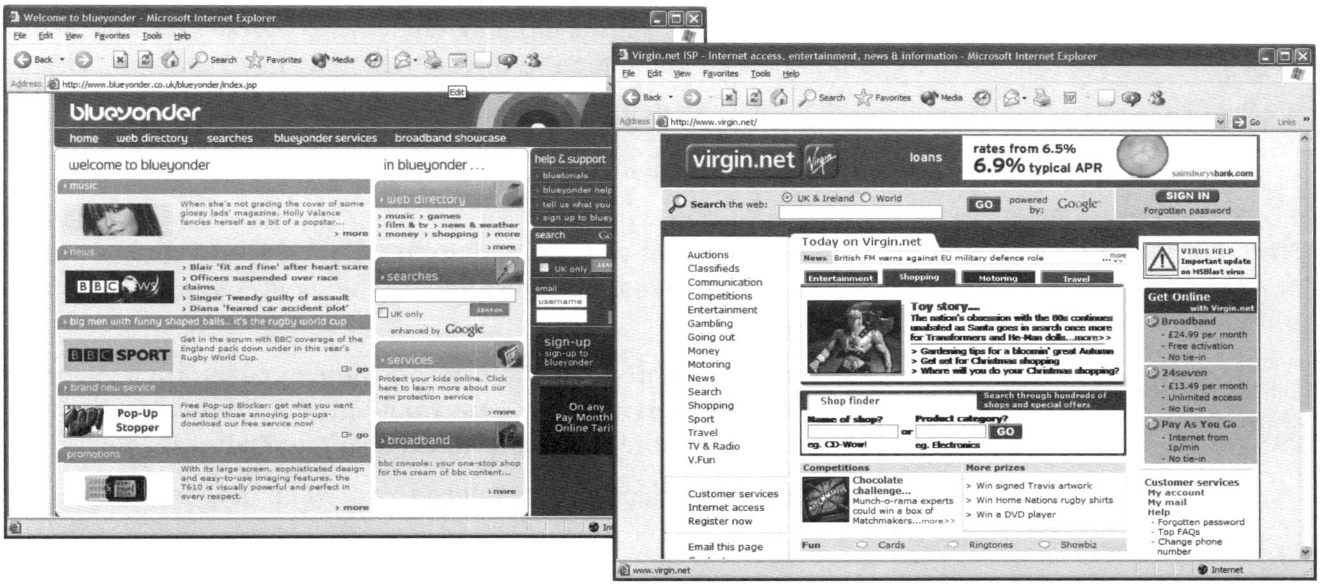

Figure 2.3 Some ISPs provide free services

Most ISPs will provide the software you need, which is already configured with all the complicated settings your computer needs to know to make the connection. It's usually only a case of putting the CD in the CD drive and following the onscreen instructions to install the software to get you up and running.

Choosing an ISP

freeserve a wanadoo company   tiscali. INTERNET WITH A PASSION.   virgin.net

Figure 2.4 Logos of various ISPs

Choosing your ISP requires some research to find the one to suit you best. The following are some of the issues you need to consider.

Costs

You can have free Internet access with most ISPs and pay just the cost of the phone calls. This can be as low as 1p per minute at weekends. You might feel that paying a monthly fee of about £10 for free access at weekends and in the evenings would be better value. Remember, if you only use the Internet at these times, you need to work out how many hours worth of surfing you could get for that monthly fee through your ordinary phone bill. It may not be quite such a good buy, unless you spend many hours on the Net. For about double that monthly fee, you might find an ISP that will give you free Internet access at any time. This might be good value if you like to spend time surfing during the day at peak call charges, or if you need to access the Net for work.

One of the benefits of free access is that if you don't think your ISP is giving a good service, you can simply change to another one. However, your e-mail account often comes with your ISP (after all, it provides you with the most important part of your address – the domain name) and changing ISPs might mean changing your e-mail address and letting everyone know. It's much the same process as when you move house, except you can use special functions in your e-mail package to send this information to everyone in your address book.

Remember:

Home-user ISPs are going to be very busy when everyone logs on to do their evening or weekend surfing and this could slow things down a bit.

Another benefit is that you can sign up to several ISPs and choose which one you use at any one time depending on the services and special offers that are available.

Because the free ISPs are geared towards the home market, they might not be able to offer the services a business would need. In this case a business would have to pay more to use a business orientated ISP.

So, there are several questions you need to ask when deciding which ISP to subscribe to.

> The first question to ask is: **Is there a subscription charge or is it free? If you have to pay, what extras do you get?**

Most ISPs will have information like that in Figure 2.5 about the service they offer. It's worth checking out a few to see what's the best option for you.

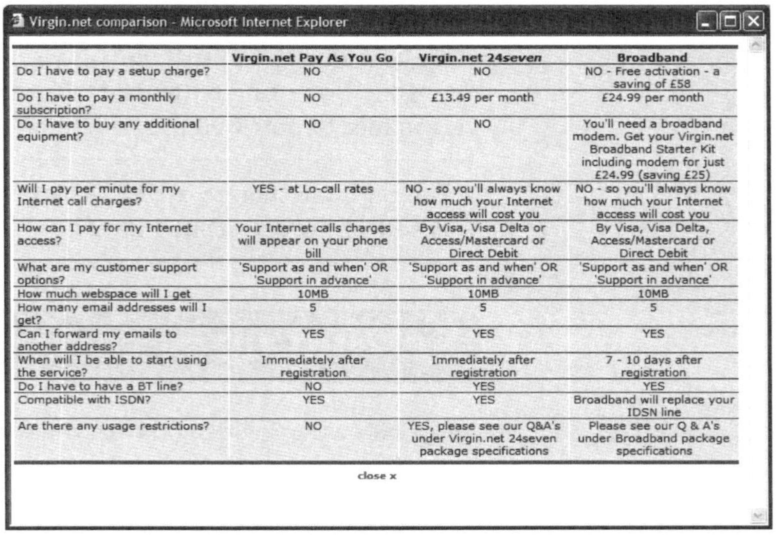

Virgin.net comparison - Microsoft Internet Explorer

	Virgin.net Pay As You Go	Virgin.net *24seven*	Broadband
Do I have to pay a setup charge?	NO	NO	NO - Free activation - a saving of £58
Do I have to pay a monthly subscription?	NO	£13.49 per month	£24.99 per month
Do I have to buy any additional equipment?	NO	NO	You'll need a broadband modem. Get your Virgin.net Broadband Starter Kit including modem for just £24.99 (saving £25)
Will I pay per minute for my Internet call charges?	YES - at Lo-call rates	NO - so you'll always know how much your Internet access will cost you	NO - so you'll always know how much your Internet access will cost you
How can I pay for my Internet access?	Your Internet calls charges will appear on your phone bill	By Visa, Visa Delta or Access/Mastercard or Direct Debit	By Visa, Visa Delta, Access/Mastercard or Direct Debit
What are my customer support options?	'Support as and when' OR 'Support in advance'	'Support as and when' OR 'Support in advance'	'Support as and when' OR 'Support in advance'
How much webspace will I get	10MB	10MB	10MB
How many email addresses will I get?	5	5	5
Can I forward my emails to another address?	YES	YES	YES
When will I be able to start using the service?	Immediately after registration	Immediately after registration	7 - 10 days after registration
Do I have to have a BT line?	NO	YES	YES
Compatible with ISDN?	YES	YES	Broadband will replace your IDSN line
Are there any usage restrictions?	NO	YES, please see our Q&A's under Virgin.net 24seven package specifications	Please see our Q & A's under Broadband package specifications

close x

Figure 2.5 ISPs provide information on the services they offer

Local connections

Most ISPs will have a **POP** (**Point of Presence**). This is a point of access to the Net. The large providers will have many POPs all over the country, which means that you should only need to dial a local number to connect with your ISP. This is important because a local POP with a local phone number will mean you will only pay local phone call charges to access the Net.

If you can connect through a local number, you can talk to other computers anywhere in the world for just the cost of a local phone call. This means you can send e-mails, files, images, etc. to Australia much cheaper than using snail mail!

> The second question to ask is: **Can I access the service via a local phone number?**

Speeding

Using your normal telephone line your modem can connect to your ISP's modem at a maximum speed of 56 Kbps (Kilobits per second). Most ISPs will support that speed of connection, but it's always worth checking. If you have something different, such as BT Home Highway or broadband, it might be a good idea to make sure that your ISP can support it.

Figure 2.6 Connection speed

If the ISP has a large number of customers all wanting to connect at the same time, you might find that you only get a busy signal and have to wait a while or try again. You could try to find out what their ratio of customer to modem is, to get an idea of how well they might be able to meet all the demands of users.

> The third question to ask is: **Do you provide access for the type and speed of modem that I have?**

Setting up

Most ISPs will provide you with the software you need to load a browser and any other necessary software. As competition between the various ISPs is so strong, most providers will have software that is already pre-configured for you. It should just be a matter of loading it and then dialling into your ISP to get your user name and password. Following the onscreen instructions should be straightforward, however most ISPs have a helpline if you get stuck. The only snag with this is that some ISPs charge a premium for their helpline service, anything up to £1 a minute, or more. This shouldn't really be necessary, but it is something you may want to bear in mind when making your choice.

> The fourth question to ask is: **Is free software included, will it be pre-configured and how much does your helpline support cost per minute?**

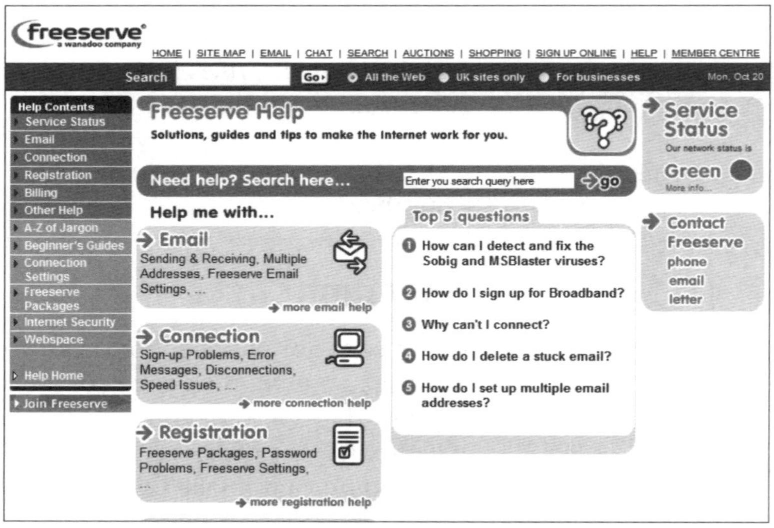

Figure 2.7 ISPs provide support for subscribers

What else?

With so many providers offering free access, you might want to find out what else they offer to subscribers. You might feel that the news services, travel information, chat rooms, etc. some providers offer are something you'd find interesting. There may be special offers at any time, such as special deals for goods or services. Would this be something you'd want to know about?

> The fifth question to ask is: **What other services do you offer?**

E-mail

E-mail packages come as standard with the two most common browsers, Internet Explorer and Netscape. If your computer is used by several members of the family, it is always preferable to have separate e-mail addresses so your messages stay private. Most providers will offer multiple e-mail addresses, but if you've a big family, the five offered by many might not be enough.

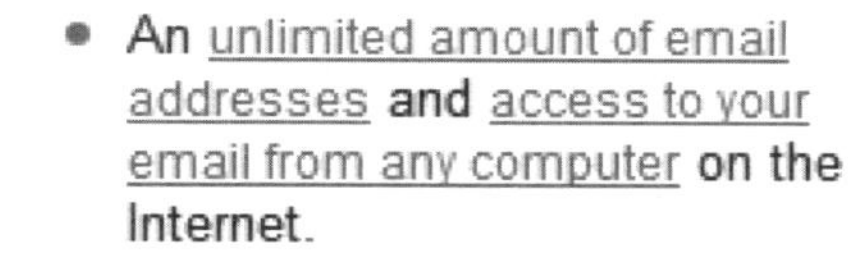

Figure 2.8 ISPs provide e-mail addresses

The sixth question to ask is: **How many e-mail addresses can I have?**

Web space

Once you get into the Net, you may decide that you would like to have your own web site. Perhaps you want to put information about your family on it so that friends and family across the country or the world can see what's happening in your life. You could put family photos, video clips, in fact anything of interest on your web site. Or you may want to set up a web site about a hobby or interest that you have, such as painting, bird watching, sports cars. To do this you will need space on a server connected to the Net, where you can upload (the opposite of download) your files. If this is something you might be interested in doing then . . .

The seventh question to ask is: **Do you include space to publish my own web pages?**

Time spent doing research into what ISPs provide may well pay dividends later if you can find the ideal ISP to suit your needs. There are several ways to find out this information:

Figure 2.9 Computer magazines are good sources of research into ISPs

- Most computer magazines have articles on ISPs from time to time. They often include a list of the most commonly available ones with information about costs, web space, numbers of customers, etc. Contact telephone numbers are often given too, if you want to phone and make your enquiries in person.
- You can use a computer connected to the Net at libraries, Internet cafés and other public Internet access machines to go to the various ISP web sites to find out the information.
- Your colleagues and friends may know about providers and give you the information you need. Often personal recommendation is the best way of choosing your ISP. After all, if they told you that such and such an ISP was slow, kept dropping the connection and was always giving a busy signal, would you take that chance?

→ Practise your skills 1

Choose an ISP accessible from the UK and find out the following information using sources available to you, e.g. computer magazines, Internet connections:

1 The **name** of the ISP.
2 The **URL** of the ISP.
3 **Local access number** (UK based, include STD code).
4 **Subscription charges** (£ sterling).
5 **Connection speed** (bits per second).
6 **Special deals** (e.g. free minutes/month, subscriber offers).
7 **Any other** information (e.g. web space available, e-mail addresses).

Getting connected

Task 2.1 Making the connection

You've chosen your preferred ISP, received the CD with the software you need, connected your modem to the computer and the telephone socket, and now is the moment to get connected.

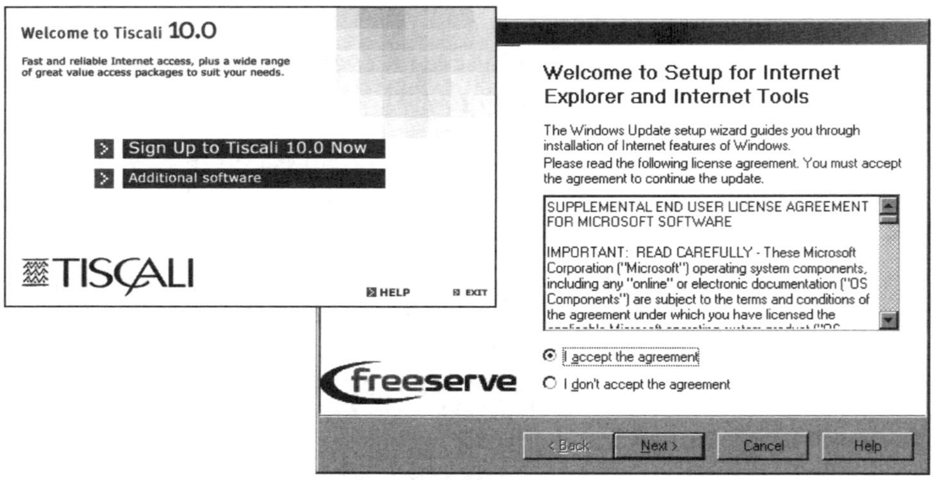

Figure 2.10 ISPs provide a CD with software to connect you to the Internet

Method

1 Switch on the computer and load the operating system.
2 Put the CD in the CD drive. Most computers are set up to automatically run (autorun) the CD when the drive tray is closed. If nothing happens, you may need to start it yourself.
Double click on **My Computer**.
Double click on the icon for your CD-ROM drive.
Double click on the icon that says **Setup**.
3 Select the **Install** option from any menus that appear in the open window. The screen may look similar to the one below.

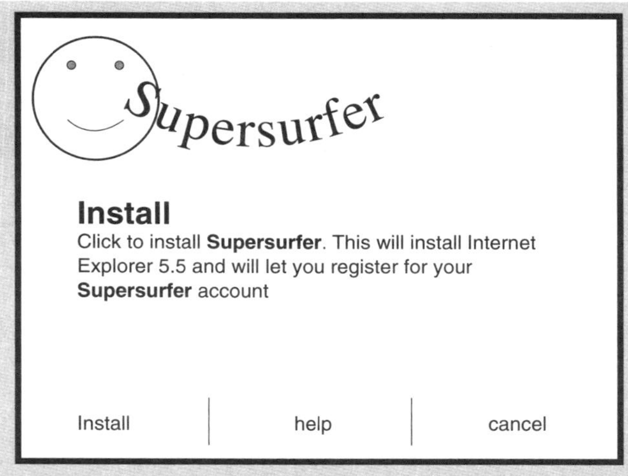

Figure 2.11 Installing software

4 If a licence agreement box appears, click on the button next to the **I accept the agreement** (you should read this first though). Click on **Next**.

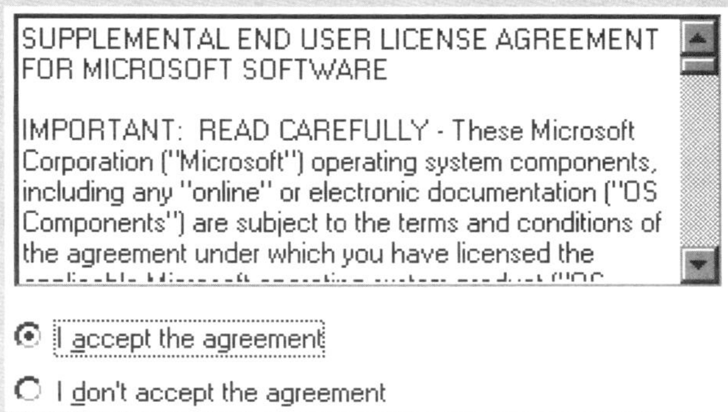

Figure 2.12 A licence agreement

5 When the software has been installed, which may take a few minutes, you will be informed that the program is going to **reset** (close down and restart) your computer. Click on the appropriate option to accept (this could be something like **Finish** or **OK**).

6 After your computer has reset, you will find the welcoming screen of your ISP, which will guide you through the setup process for your account. Follow the instructions on screen, which may look something like this:

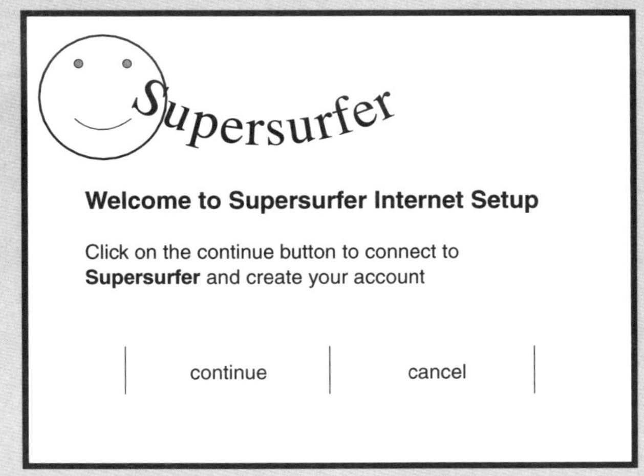

Figure 2.13 The sort of screen that welcomes you to an ISP

7 At some point you will need to enter some personal details and make your choice of e-mail address and password. The screen may look similar to the one shown, but will be individual for each provider.

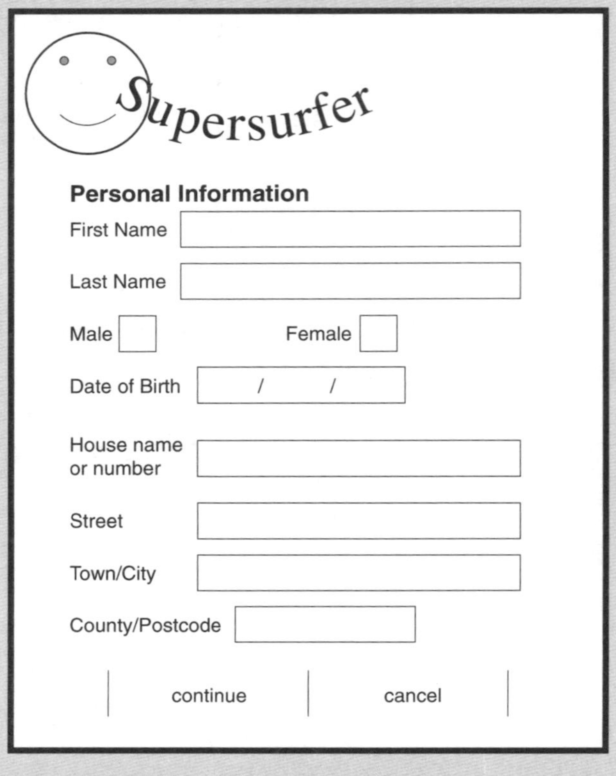

Figure 2.14 A screen like this shows information needed to set up an e-mail address and password

8 Your computer may dial up your new ISP to complete the registration procedure. Don't worry about the strange screeching noises your modem might make – it's just part of the connection process.

9 Once all the signing up is done, you can access your browser by double clicking on the appropriate icon on your desktop. This may be the Internet Explorer icon 

or the Netscape icon , or it may be an icon which your ISP provides through their software.

Remember:

You may need to choose your modem from a dialogue box.

Remember:

Don't forget to make a note of your e-mail address and your password. You might be reminded by the software, but make sure that you keep your password safe from other eyes.

Information

When you choose your e-mail address, you may find that you will have to make a second choice if someone else has already chosen the one you want. If your name is John Smith, you can imagine that there are probably quite a few such John Smiths who have asked for j.smith as their e-mail name! It's a good idea to have a few other suggestions ready, just in case.

Going online

Task 2.2 Connecting to your new ISP

Method

1. Double click on your **browser** icon.
2. Enter your password in the dialogue box which appears.

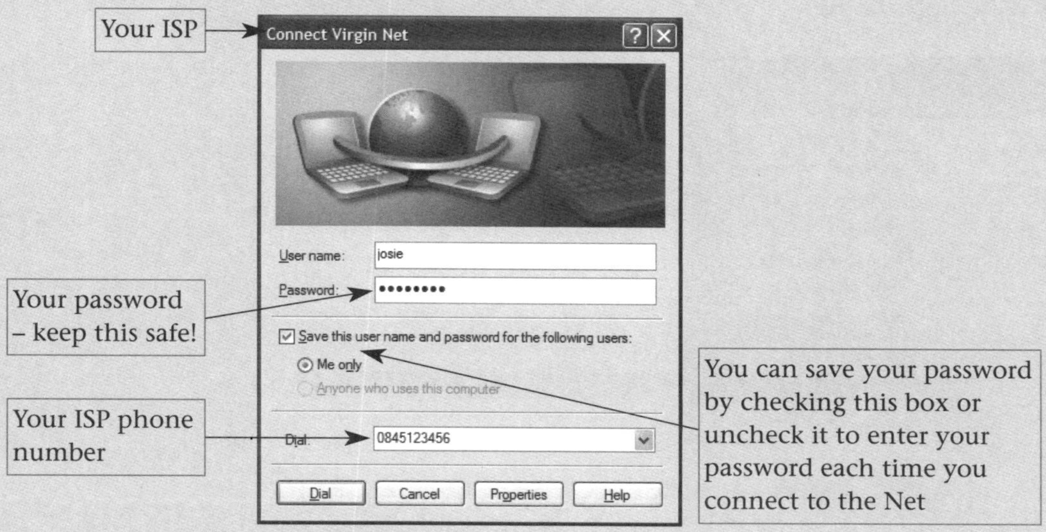

Figure 2.15 Connecting to an ISP

3. Click on **Dial.** Your modem will make those strange squealing sounds as it dials and connects.
4. If communication is established with your ISP, the **Connected** icon will appear on your taskbar. This will flash as data is transferred from the Net to your computer and vice-versa.
5. Your provider's homepage should appear, although you can select which page you want to use as your starting page at a later date.

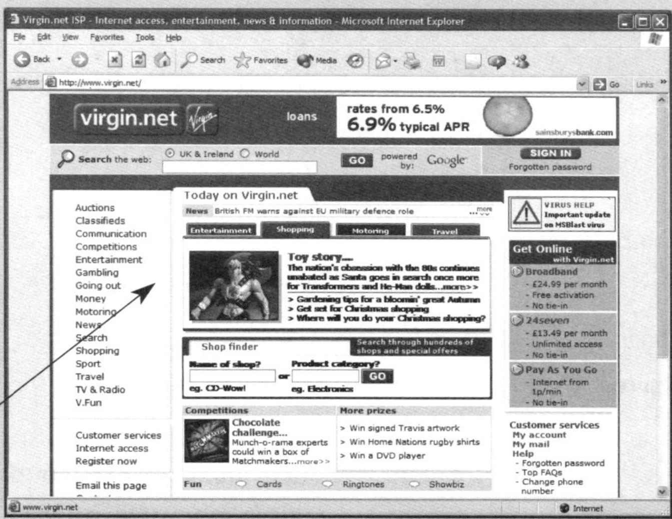

Figure 2.16 Virgin's homepage

Remember:

Homepage can mean the page your browser displays when it first starts or it can be the first page of a web site.

Information

If you have a broadband connection, which is 'always on', i.e. a permanent connection to the Internet, you will only need to double click on your browser icon to reach your homepage.

Task 2.3 Changing your homepage

Method

1. Click on **Start**.
2. Navigate the menu and select **Control Panel**.
3. Double click on the **Internet Options**.
4. Select the **General** tab.
5. Enter the URL of the web page you want as your homepage.
6. Click on **Apply** and **OK**.

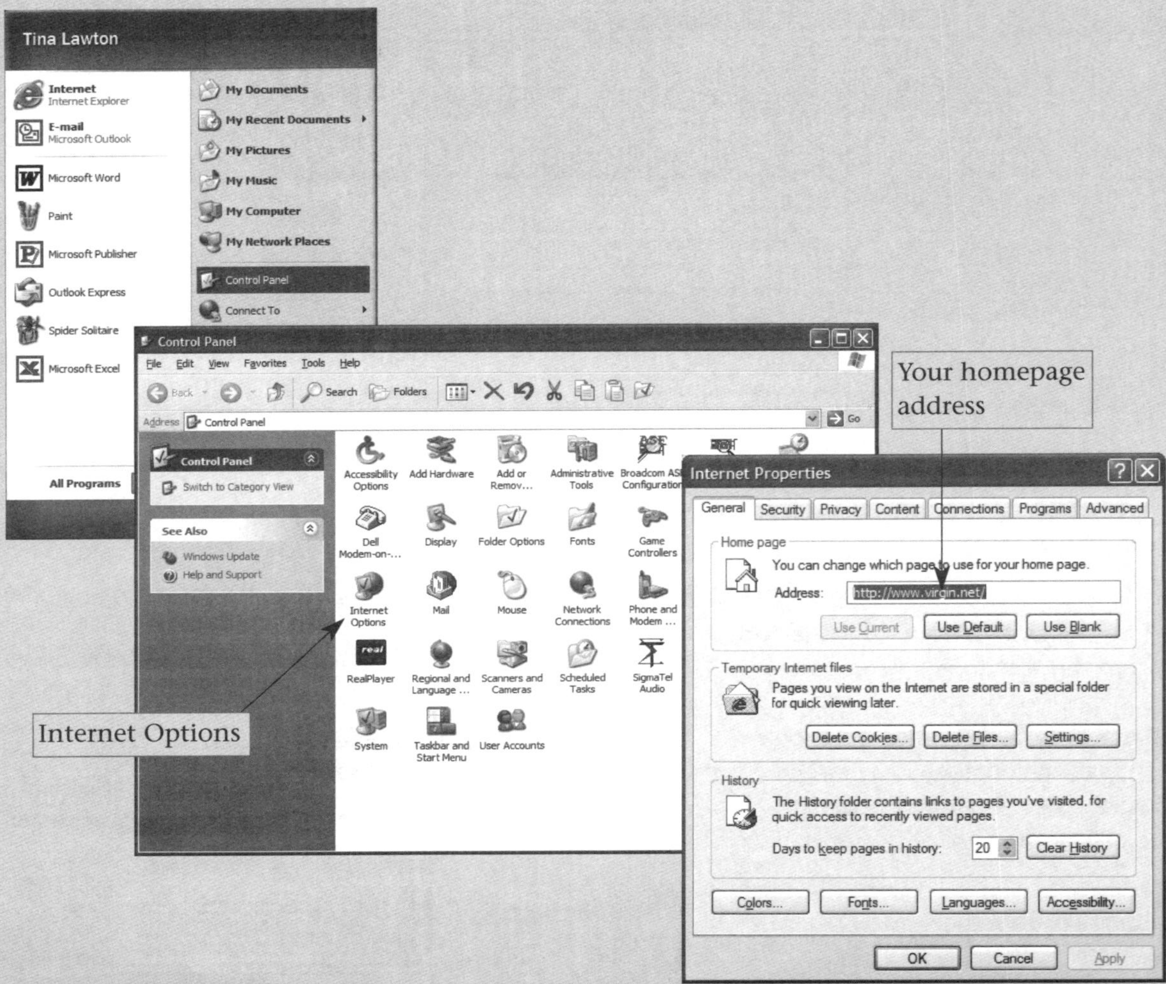

Figure 2.17 The options for changing your homepage

Hint:

If you make changes to your Internet Properties but decide that you don't want to '**Apply**' the changes, you can always click on the **Cancel** button, which will leave the settings as they were before you began.

There are many other options you can choose from to set up your Internet connection to suit yourself, and some of these will be looked at in later sections.

Now you're ready to explore the Internet and discover a whole new world of information and entertainment.

→ Practise your skills 2

1 Using the seven questions to consider when choosing an ISP, draw up a table to record information about three different ISPs.

Research your information and enter the data in your table.

2 Which ISP would you choose out of the three you have researched? Give reasons for your answer.

→ Check your knowledge

1 What is the difference between an Online Service and an ISP?

2 What services might an ISP provide?

3 Briefly explain what questions you need to ask yourself when choosing an ISP?

4 Why is a local Point of Presence important when deciding on an ISP?

5 Why might you want more than one e-mail address?

6 At what speed does your modem connect to the Internet?

7 What does bps stand for?

8 What do you need to connect to the Internet?

9 Why should you read the ISP's licence agreement before accepting it?

10 What is a homepage?

Section 3 'Surfing' the Net

You will learn to

- Navigate web pages and hotspots to locate sites
  - ☐ Exit a browser and disconnect
- Use URLs to locate sites
- Create Favorites (Bookmarks) of visited URLs
  - ☐ Use Favorites (Bookmarks) to reload web pages
- Use forward, back and past site history to locate sites
- Save web pages
  - ☐ Locate and retrieve saved documents
- Download information from a site
- Identify the purpose of a search engine
- Locate and select search engines
- Use search engines to find typical services
  - ☐ One word
  - ☐ Several words
  - ☐ "quote marks"
  - ☐ + and − signs
  - ☐ type in question
- Use directories to search for information
- Use meta searches
- Print web pages

Web pages

When you've loaded your browser and connected to the Net, your **homepage** should appear in the open window. This may be the homepage of your ISP, or one that you've chosen yourself, but a browser will always open at a page of some sort even if it's to tell you that it can't find the page you want!

The screen shots in this unit have been taken using Internet Explorer, but the functions in Netscape are very similar.

The example shown on the next page is the BBCi Homepage. From here you will be able to access all the information and ideas about the many topics developed to entertain and inform you. You can learn more about the programmes on the BBC, find out what's going on in your favourite soaps and get up-to-the-minute sports news, as well as help to study and revise for exams. Most such sites are set up to make access to this content as easy as possible.

Your screen should look something like the one shown below:

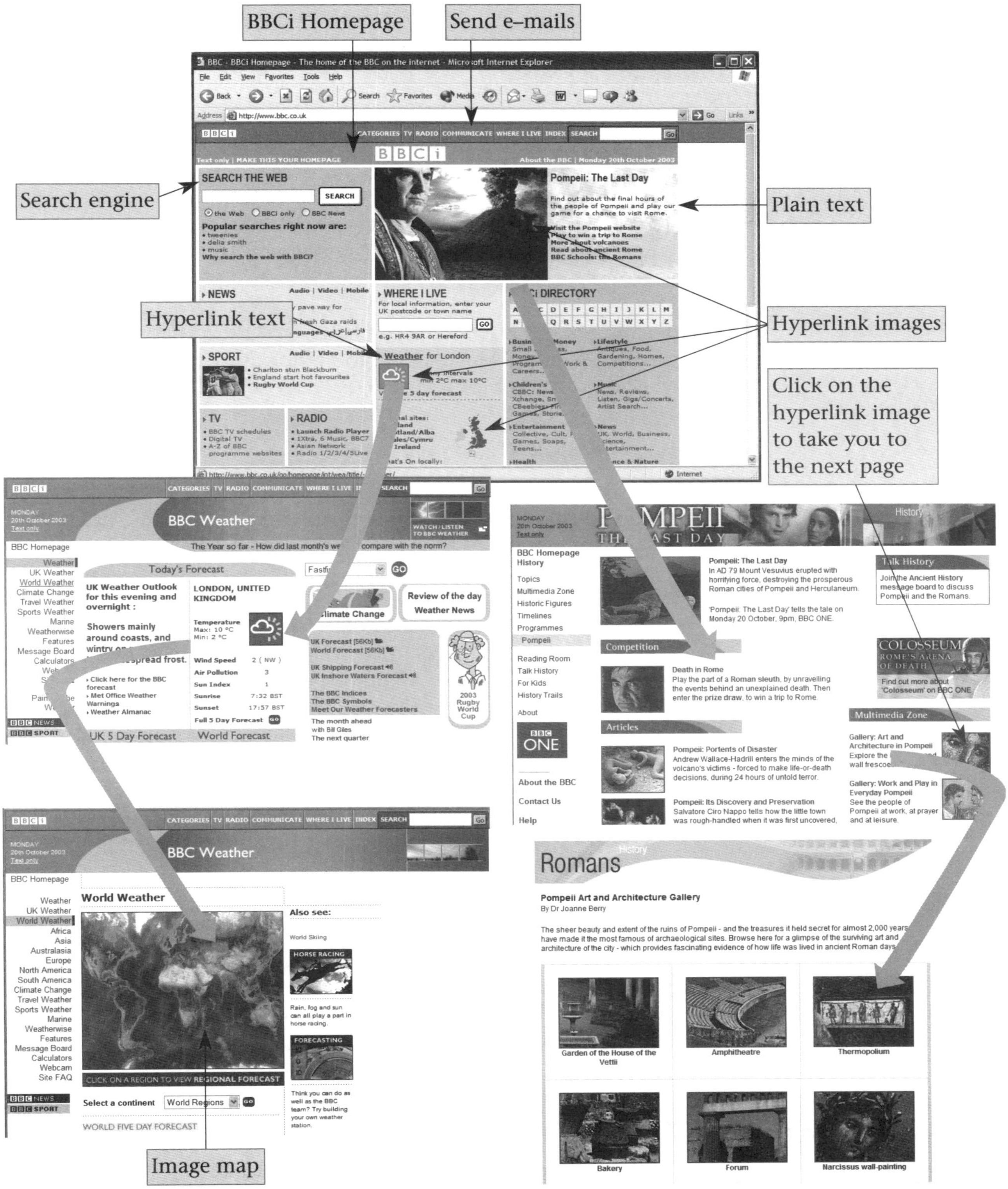

Figure 3.1 Web pages

Many web pages will have a mix of text and images on them. Some of the text may have lines underneath and some of the images may change or move as you pass your mouse pointer over them. These are **hyperlinks** (also called **hotspots**) which are used to link to other pages. Your mouse pointer will change to a hand with a pointing finger as you move it over the hyperlinks. If you click on one of these links you will find another page opens. Following hyperlinks in this way can lead you from your own computer to a page halfway across the world. Hotspots on web pages can lead you anywhere!

Information

A web site can be made up of just one page – perhaps with some information and a few pictures – to the hundreds of pages a company might have showing you all their products.

Hyperlinks don't just open other web pages, they could play a video clip or a sound file, download an application, run a program, show a picture – in fact, many different things – you just have to click on them to find out what happens.

On a web page you may find:

- **Plain text** Ordinary text. Clicking on this will do nothing at all!
- **Hyperlink text** A text link to another page which could be on the same web site or on another computer anywhere in the world. Hypertext links are nearly always underlined, although they can be in any font or colour.
- **Image** A picture or graphic that makes the web site look interesting and colourful. Although an image might be useful to illustrate something, clicking on it won't take you anywhere.
- **Hyperlinked image** Clicking on this link will open a new page. It probably won't look any different to any other image, but don't forget that your mouse pointer will change to a hand when you pass it over a hyperlinked image.
- **Image map** This is an image made up of smaller images, such as a map of Britain, where different parts of the map will take you to information about each county.
- **E-mail link** You can use this link to open your e-mail program and send a message to the address automatically placed in the address box.

This clicking on hyperlinks can take you a long way from home, and you may find that you've suddenly become lost. The **toolbar** in Explorer is your way home – literally. Clicking on the **Home** button on the toolbar will take you back to where you began – your homepage.

Remember:

Homepage can mean the page your browser displays when it first starts or it can be the first page of a web site.

→ Practise your skills 1

1 Load your browser and connect to your ISP.
2 Begin to explore the Net using the hyperlinks on your homepage.
3 Click the **Home** button to return to your homepage.

More about the toolbar

It's well worth getting to know your toolbar to find out the many functions it can perform. It can save you a lot of time and hassle when you're surfing the Net!

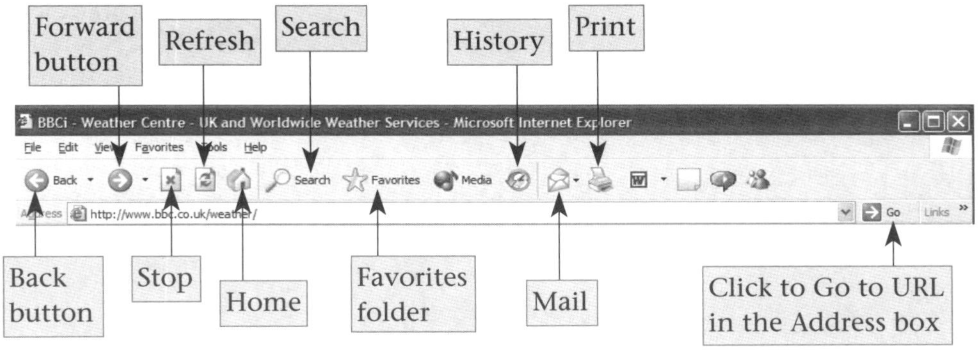

Figure 3.2 The toolbar

- **Back** Clicking this button will take you back to the last page you visited. Keep clicking and you can work your way backwards through all the pages you've been to.
- **Forward** If you have used the Back button to view a page you've been to before, you can use this button to return to a page you've already visited. If you have not used the Back button, this button will be greyed-out.
- **Stop** This button stops the page from loading. This can be useful if you find a page is taking too long to load and you don't want to wait, or if you find a page appearing that you didn't want.
- **Refresh** Click this button to reload the same page again. This is sometimes necessary if there is a problem and the page doesn't load properly or doesn't load at all!
- **Home** This takes you back to your homepage – useful if you get lost or want to start again.
- **Search** This opens another window where you can enter keywords or topics and search for web pages which might have the information you need. (More about searching later.)
- **Favorites** This button will give you a list of all the sites you visit often. You can add sites or delete sites from this list. It's a bit like an address book, and can save you a lot of time – after all, who can remember all those words and dots which make up your favourite site addresses?
- **History** All the pages you've visited recently are listed here. You can go back to any page in your history by clicking on the URL.
- **Mail** Opens your e-mail program.
- **Print** Prints the web page in view.

Remember:

There are other options available for your toolbar which you can access from the **Tools** menu by selecting **Options**.

Task 3.1 Exiting and disconnecting

When you have finished your surfing session, you should **exit** your browser and **disconnect** from the Net. This is very important if you are paying for the connection call from home – otherwise your phone bill might be rather large!

To exit and disconnect from the Net:

Method

1 Click on the **Close** option in the **File** menu.

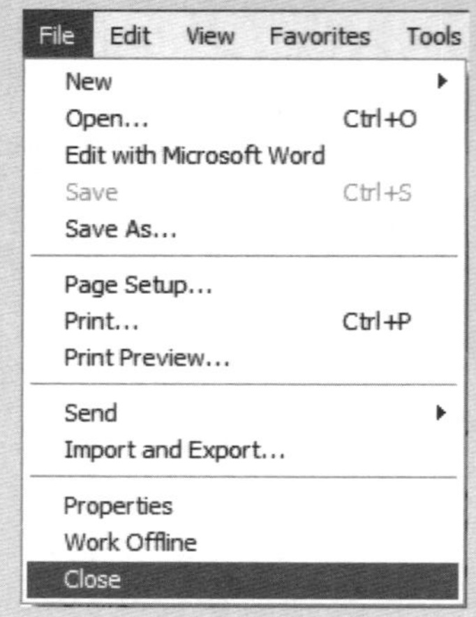

Figure 3.3 Close

2 Right mouse click on the **Connected** icon on your taskbar and select **Disconnect** from the pop-up menu.

Figure 3.4 Choosing Disconnect from the pop-up menu

Using URLs

A **Uniform Resource Locator (URL)** is the Internet address of a particular web page. These addresses begin with **http://** followed by **www** to indicate that it's a page on the World Wide Web.

Web addresses will look something like this example:

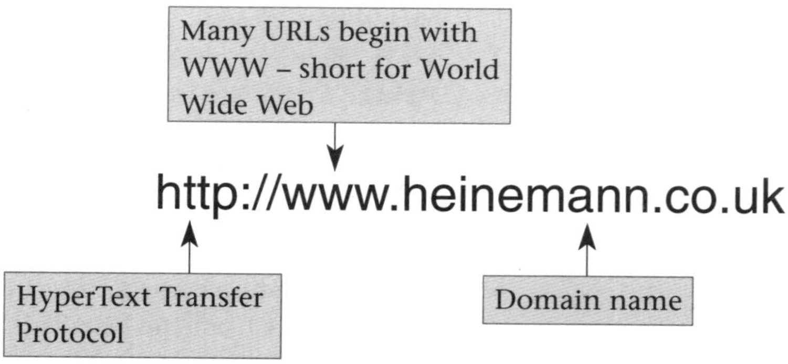

Hint:

Don't forget to type any web addresses exactly as they are written – no spaces and watch the dots!

Task 3.2 Loading a web page knowing the URL of the page you want to view

Method

1 Click in the browser's **Address** bar.
2 Enter the URL of the web page you want to view.
3 Press the **Enter** key on the keyboard.

→ Practise your skills 2

1 Load your browser software and connect to your ISP.
2 Enter the URL http://www.bbc.co.uk in the address bar.
3 Navigate the web pages to identify the programme on BBC 1 tonight at 9.00 pm.
4 Use the Back button to return to the BBC homepage.
5 Click on the Home button to return to your homepage.
6 Enter the URL http://www.channel4.co.uk in the address bar.
7 Navigate the web pages to identify the programme on Channel 4 tonight at 9.00 pm.
8 Use the Back button to return to the web site homepage.
9 Use the Forward button to return to the second page you visited on the web site. Note down the URL.
10 Return to your homepage.
11 Exit your browser and disconnect.

Remember:

This facility is called **Bookmarks** or **Hotlists** in some other browsers.

Remember:

You will need to be online and be at the page you wish to add to your Favorites folder, although you can organise your folders later when you are offline.

My Favorites (Bookmarks)

You can put your favourite web site addresses in your **Favorites** folder. (The spelling is American – hence the missing 'u'!) This is a very handy tool in Explorer and can save you a lot of time finding any interesting web sites that you want to go back to.

If you have added a site to your **Favorites** you can go to it with a single click.

Task 3.3 Adding a web page address to your Favorites

Method 1

1. Find the page you want to add.
2. Click on the **Favorites** item on the menu bar.
3. Select **Add to Favorites** from the drop down menu.
4. In the dialogue box which appears you can click in the **Name:** box and enter the name you want to call the page or accept the suggested name.
5. Click on **OK**.

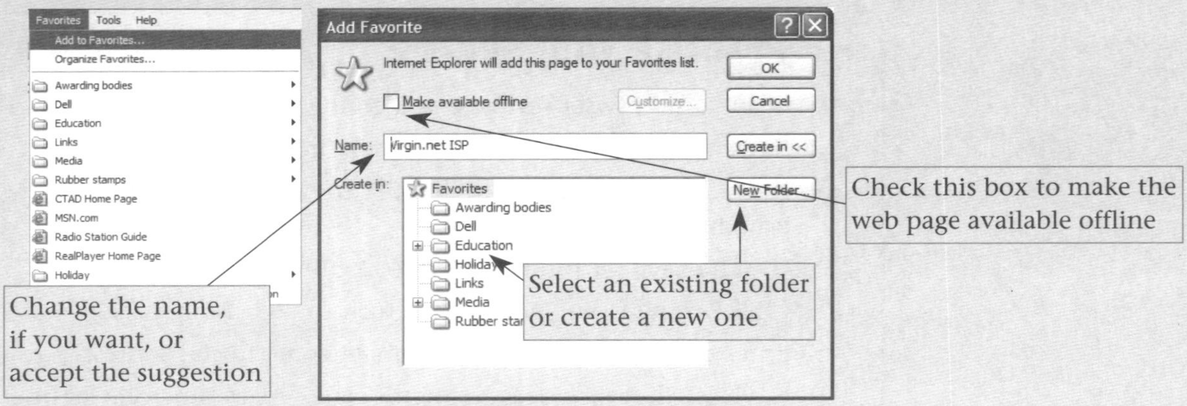

Figure 3.5 One method of adding web pages to a Favorites folder

Method 2

1. Find the page you want to add.
2. Right click the mouse button and a pop-up menu appears.
3. Move down the menu to select **Add to Favorites**.
4. In the dialogue box which appears you can click in the **Name:** box and enter the name you want to call the page or accept the suggested name.
5. Click on **OK**.

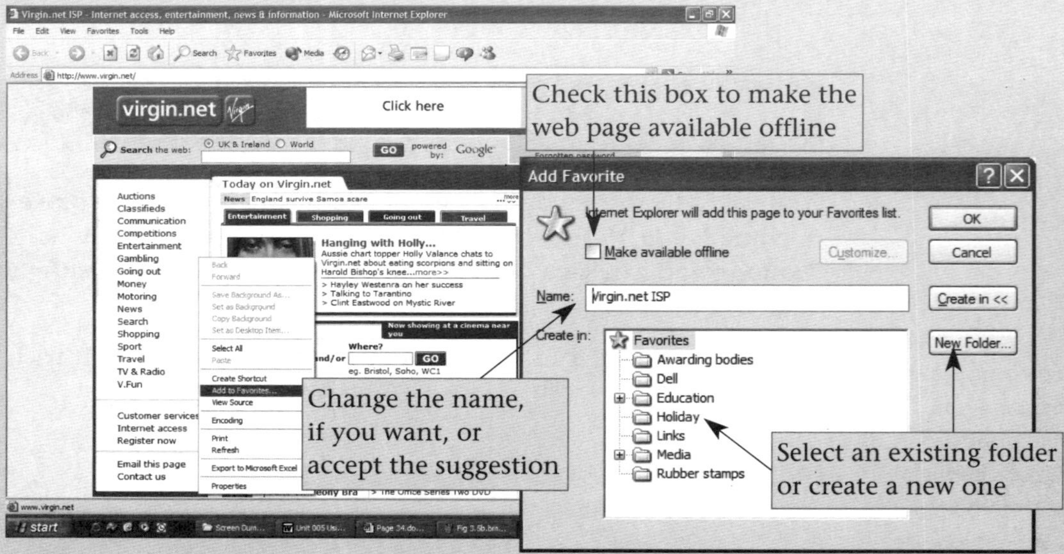

Figure 3.6 Another method of adding web pages to the Favorites folder

If you've got lots of favourite web pages which you've added to your Favorites folder, you'll soon find that they need to be organised to make it easier to find the one you want. You can do this by creating new folders and putting similar web page addresses together into the folders. You could have folders for Music, Jobs, News, Travel, and Shopping, for example.

Task 3.4 Organising your Favorites

Method 1

1 Select **Organize** (American spelling, again!) **Favorites** from the **Favorites** menu.
2 Select the **Create Folder** option from the dialogue box which appears.
3 A new folder will appear and you can enter the name you want to call the folder.
4 Select the address you want to place in the folder and click on the **Move to Folder** button.
5 Select the appropriate folder from the list in the dialogue box which appears.
6 Click on **OK**.
7 Click on **Close**.

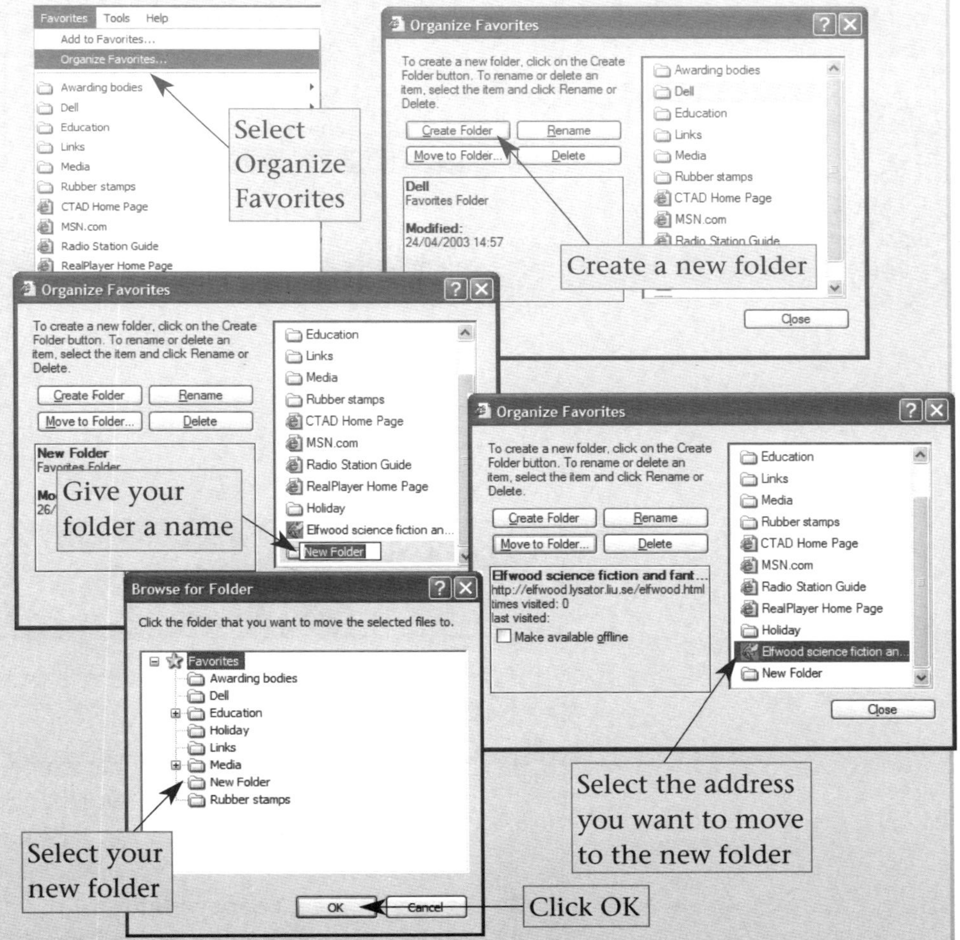

Figure 3.7 One method of organising Favorites

Method 2

1 Click on the **Favorites** item on the menu bar.
2 A split pane showing the contents of your Favorites folder will appear on the left-hand side.
3 Click on **Organize** from the options at the top of the pane.
4 Follow steps 2–7 as shown in Method 1.

You can repeat this to move all your web addresses into their appropriate folders.

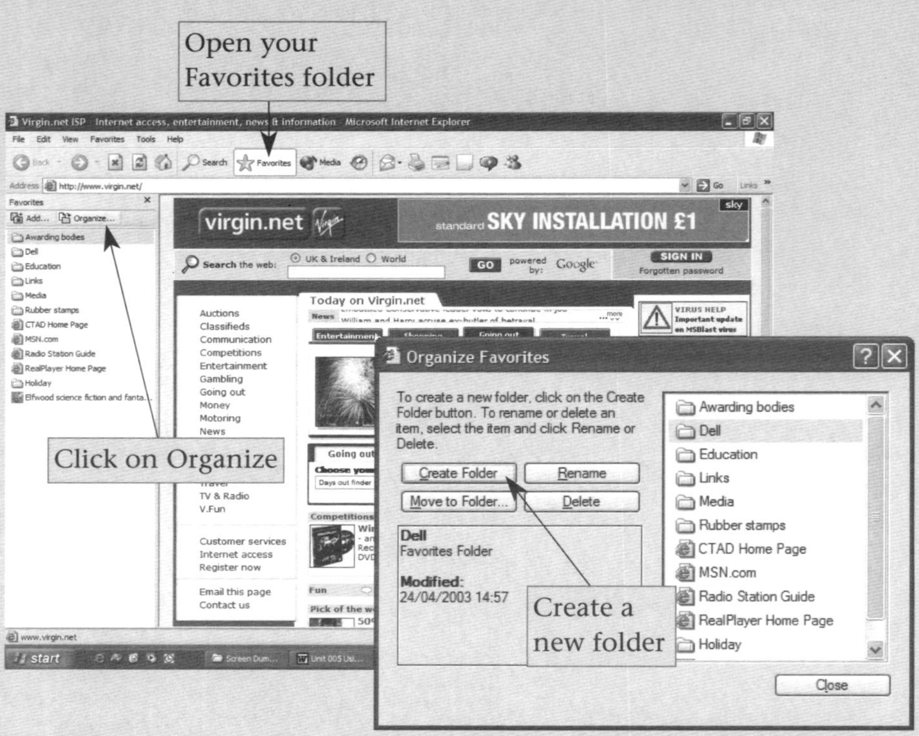

Figure 3.8 Another method of organising Favorites

Hint:

If you have a folder in your Favorites already, you may want to put a new web address straight into it.

Task 3.5 Adding an address to a particular folder in your Favorites

Method

1 Use either the right mouse button or the Favorites item on the menu bar to select the **Add to Favorites** option as before.
2 In the dialogue box which appears, enter the name or accept the suggestion.
3 Click on the **Create in** button.
4 Select the appropriate folder from the list which appears.
5 Click on **OK**.

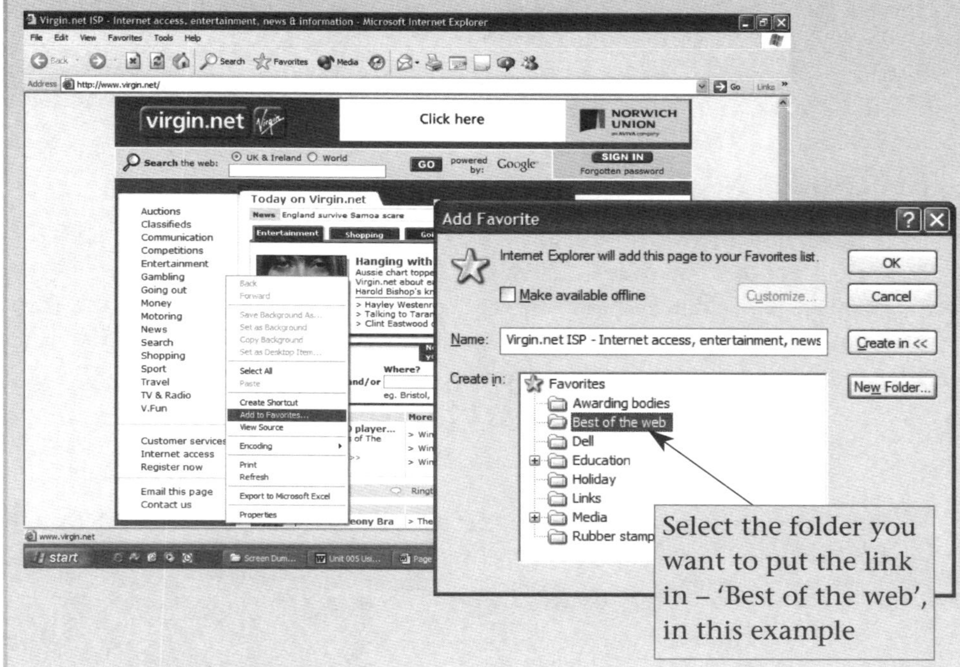

Figure 3.9 Adding an address to a folder in Favorites

→ Practise your skills 3

1. Load your browser and connect to your ISP.
2. Find the BBC web page. (**Remember**: Type the URL into the address box and press **Enter** on your keyboard.)
3. Use one of the above methods to add the web page address to your Favorites folder. Name the address BBC.
4. Create a new folder in your Favorites. Call the folder **TV Channels**.
5. Move the BBC favourite into the TV Channels folder.
6. Find the Channel 4 web page and add this directly to your TV Channel folder.
7. Disconnect and close your browser.

Weblinks:

To access the web site content relevant to this page visit www.heinemann.co.uk/hotlinks

Enter express code 2733P, click GO and then click on the relevant link from the text.

Now you've got your favourite sites organised, you can load the page with a single click.

Hint:

If you have entered a URL in the Address box, you can also click the **Go** button → Go to the right of the Address box to go to the web page.

Task 3.6 Loading a page from your Favorites folder

Method

1. Load your browser and connect to your ISP.
2. Click on the **Favorites** button on the toolbar.
3. Select the folder and then the address for the web page you want from the list.
4. To close the Favorites pane, click on the **Favorites** button on the toolbar again.
5. Disconnect and close your browser.

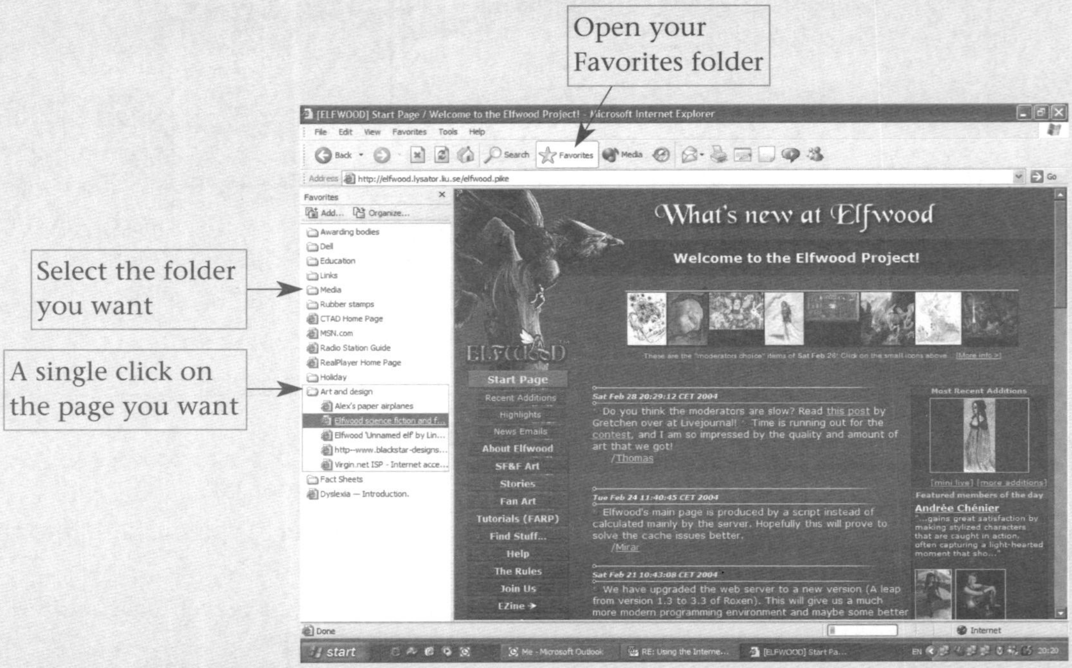

Figure 3.10 Loading a page from a Favorites folder

Information

As time passes, you may find that some of the web addresses in your Favorites folder are no longer available or you may not want to keep them as a Favorite item any more. You can use the **Delete** button in the **Organize** dialogue box. You can also **Rename** addresses and folders from this dialogue box by selecting the **Rename** button.

The past is History!

It may be tempting to add lots of web sites to your Favorites, but it's worth being selective, otherwise you could end up with too many folders and addresses to find what you want quickly. However, it may be that you visited a web site recently and didn't add it to your Favorites, but realise that you do want to visit it again to check something or to find out a vital piece of information. All is not lost – the **History** list will give you a handy way of finding that elusive web site.

Explorer keeps this list of sites visited automatically, and just a single click on the **History** button on the toolbar will bring a split pane on the left-hand side of the screen, much like the Favorites pane, showing exactly where you've been over the last couple of weeks.

Task 3.7 Finding a recently visited site from the History folder

Method

1. Click on the **History** button on the toolbar.
2. Select the week and day (if you can remember!) when you visited the web site last. If you can't remember the exact week and day, you may have to have a few tries at finding it.
3. Select the site you want from the list which opens.
4. If you're connected to the Net, the web page should load.

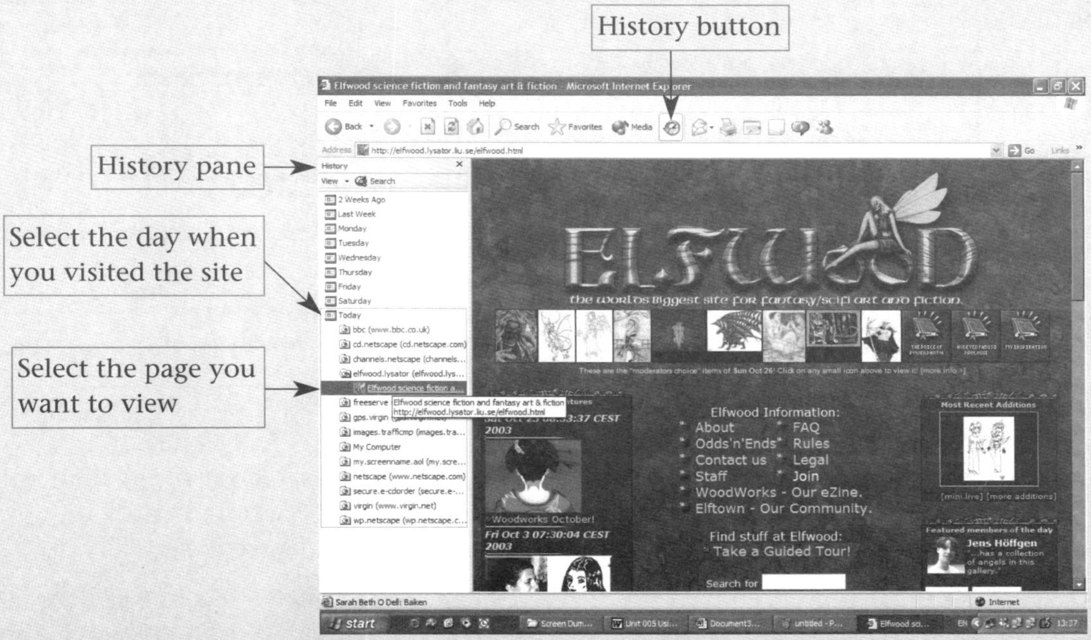

Figure 3.11 Finding a site from the History folder

Task 3.8 Setting the length of time pages are stored in History

You can change the length of time your pages are stored in History by setting the options to suit you.

Method 1

1 Select **Control Panel** from the **Start** menu.
2 Select **Internet Options** from the Control Panel window.
3 Make sure the **General** tab is selected and use the up and down arrow keys in the **History** section to change the length of time.
4 Click on **Apply** and then **OK** to accept the changes.

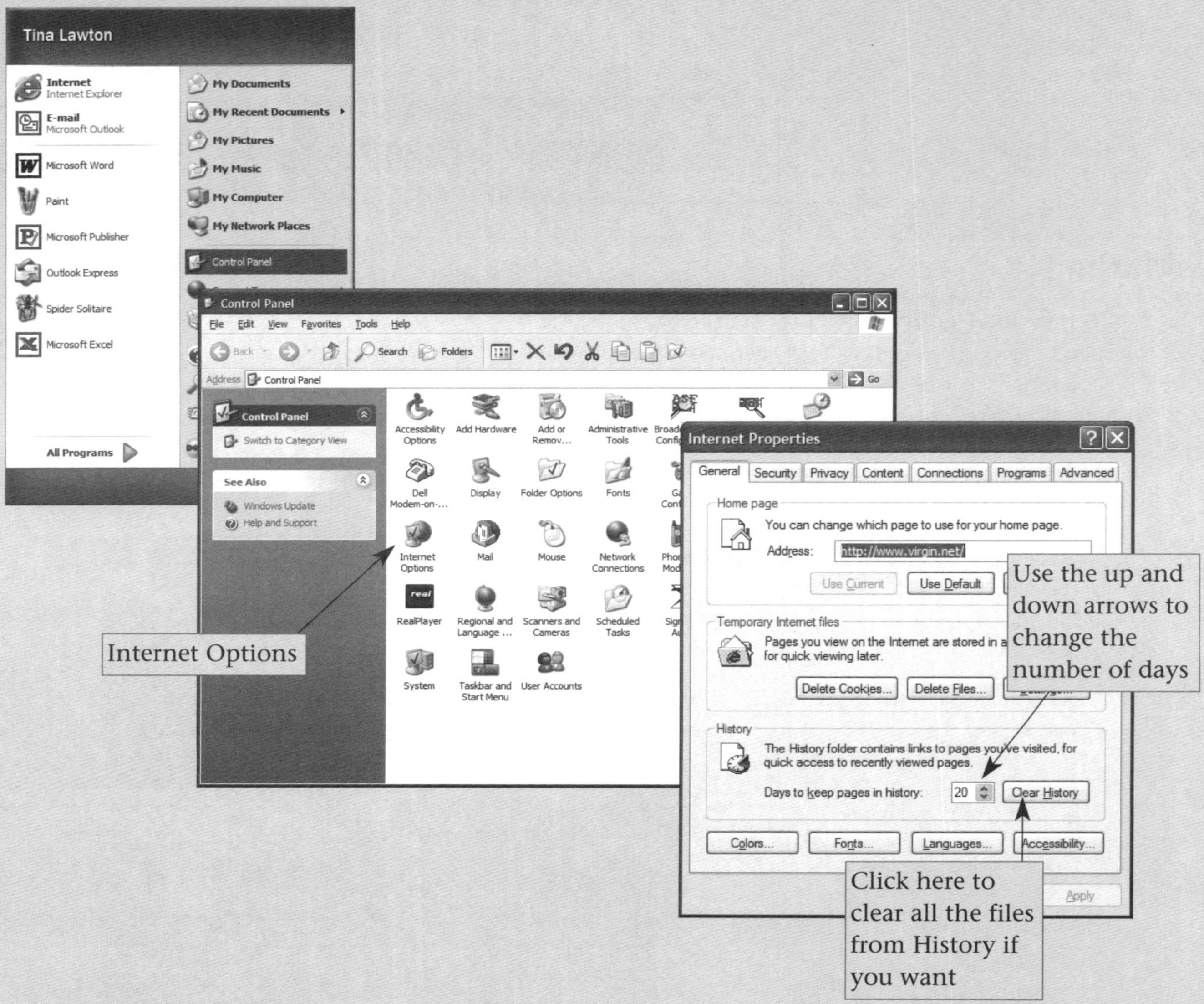

Figure 3.12 One method of setting length of time to store pages in History

Hint:

You can also clear all the information stored in History by clicking the **Clear History** button in this box.

Method 2

1. Select **Tools** from the menu bar.
2. Select **Internet Options** from the drop down menu.
3. Make sure the **General** tab is selected and use the up and down arrow keys in the **History** section to change the length of time.
4. Click on **Apply** and then **OK** to accept the changes.

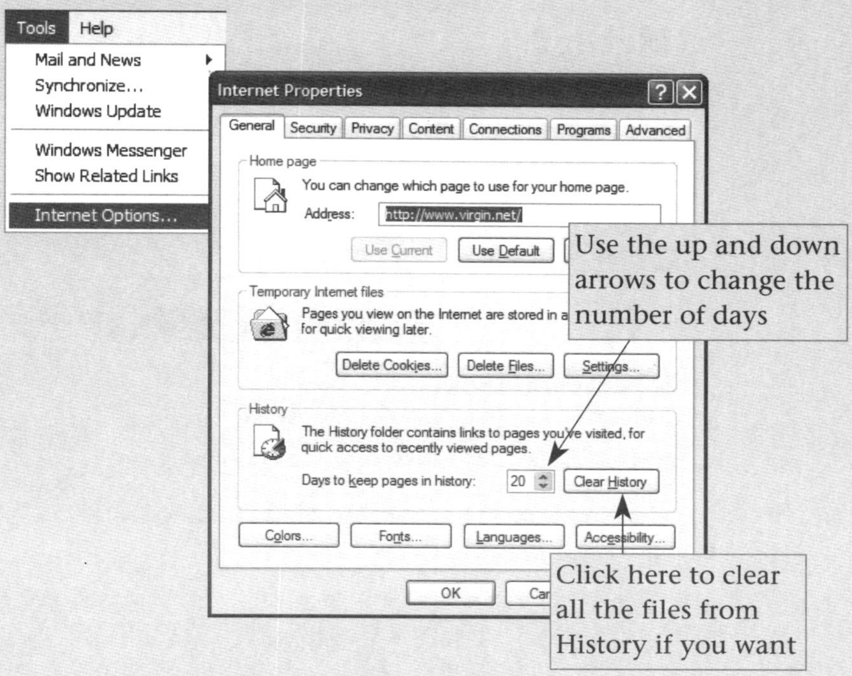

Figure 3.13 Another method of setting length of time to store pages in History

→ Practise your skills 4

1. Load your browser and connect to your ISP.
2. Open your History folder.
3. Select the day when you visited the BBC or Channel 4 web site.
4. Select one of these pages.
5. Take a screen shot of the loaded web page.
6. Paste into a new word processing document and print out a copy.
7. Find out and note down how many days pages are left in your History folder.
8. Disconnect and close your browser.

Saving information

One of the exciting things about the Web is the huge amount of data and information stored on web sites across the world. There is bound to come a time when you want to save some of this information to look at or use at a later date. You can save information to your hard drive, or even a floppy disk, so that you always have it to hand. The information you might want to save could be text, images, video clips, music files, programs – a whole range of things.

Task 3.9 Saving text that is displayed in your browser window

You can save the text on a web page to paste into another document later, or to print out and read at your leisure.

Method

1. Open the **File** menu on the toolbar and select the **Save File As** option.
2. Select **Text File** from the **Save as type** list box.
3. Enter your chosen filename in the **File name** box.
4. Select the location where you want to save the file and click **Save**.

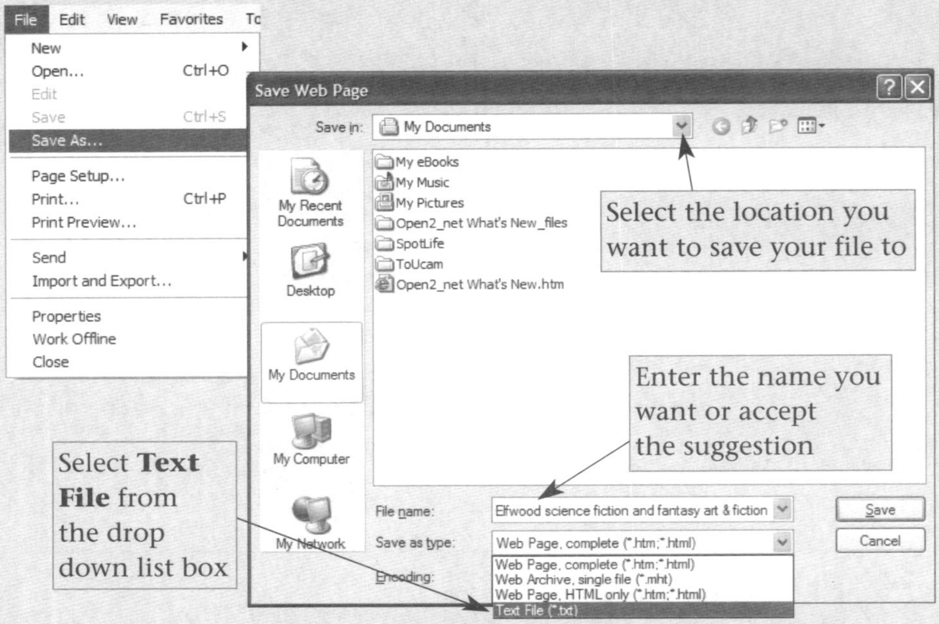

Figure 3.14 Saving text from a web page

> **Hint:**
> If you only want to save a small part of the text, highlight the text you want and save as above. You could also do this and copy to the clipboard if you wanted to paste it into a document straight away.

Task 3.10 Saving a web page

You might want to save more than just the text on a web page; you might want the images as well.

Hint:

If you saved the web page as HTML in the **Save as type** list box, you would keep the same layout but would have icons in the place of the pictures.

Hint:

You can also save your image as wallpaper from this menu.

Method

1 Open the **File** menu on the toolbar and select the **Save File As** option.
2 Select **Web Page, complete** from the **Save as type** list box.
3 Enter your chosen filename in the **File name** box.
4 Select the location where you want to save the file and click **Save**.

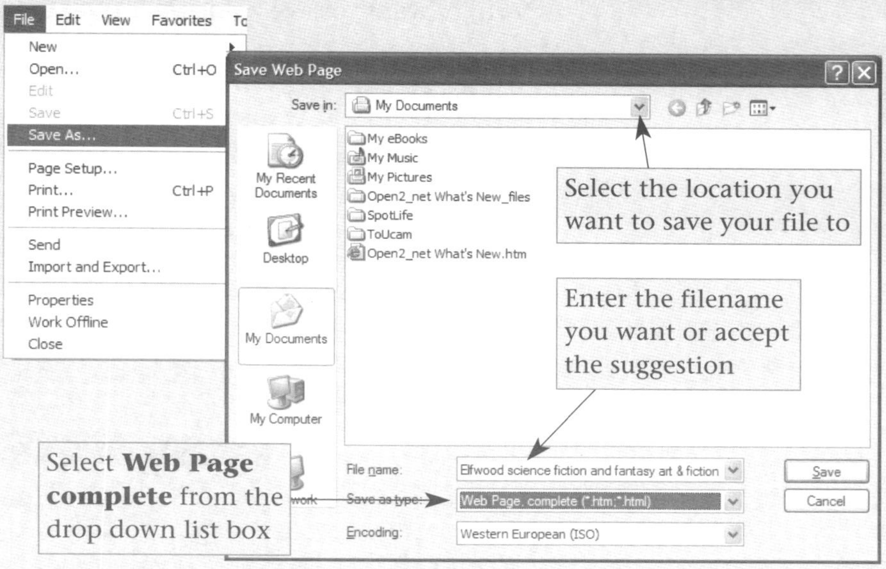

Figure 3.15 Saving a web page

Task 3.11 Saving an image on a web page

Sometimes you might just want to save a picture from a web page. If you want to save more than one picture on a web page, you will have to save each picture individually.

Method

1 Place your mouse pointer over the image and use your right mouse button to access the pop-up menu.
2 Select **Save Picture As** from the menu.
3 Enter your chosen filename in the **File name** box.
4 Select the location where you want to save the file and click **Save**.

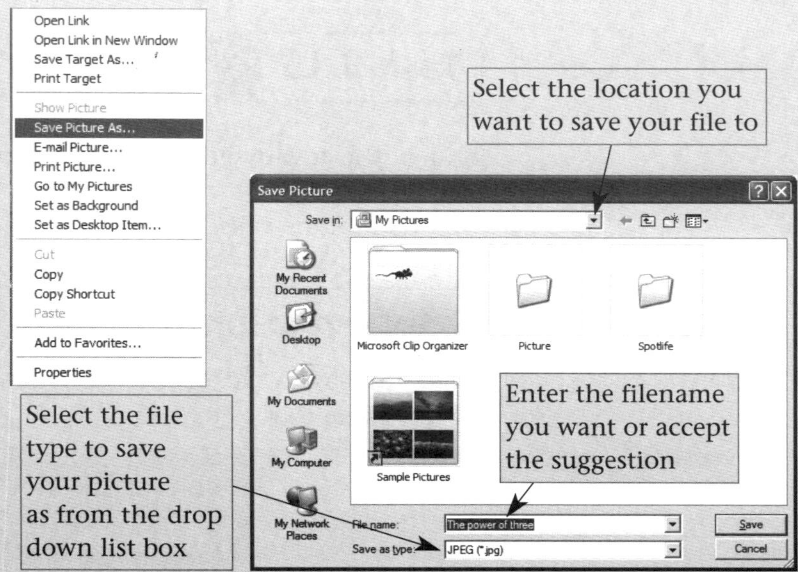

Figure 3.16 Saving an image on a web page

Task 3.12 Saving a link or a document

You can use a hyperlink to save a web page or a document without having to display the page in your browser window. This may be useful if you want to save several pages from a web site without having to load each page in turn, or want to save a document to read later.

Method

1 Place your mouse pointer over the hyperlink and use your right mouse button to access the pop-up menu.
2 Select **Save Target As** from the menu.
3 Enter your chosen filename in the **File name** box.
4 Select the location where you want to save the file and click **Save**.

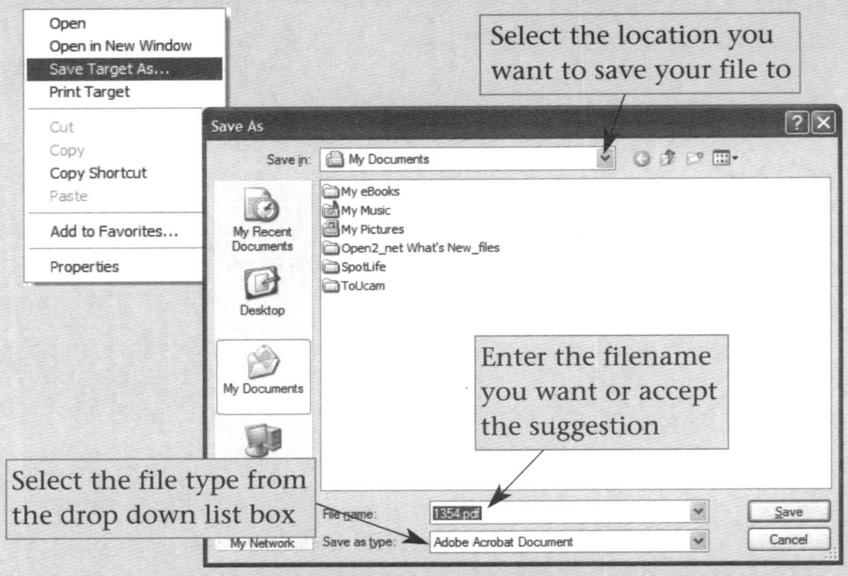

Figure 3.17 Saving a link

Task 3.13 Viewing your saved information

One of the advantages of saving information to your hard disk is that you can view it at any time without having to connect to the Net again. This saves on phone calls!

Information

If you have a broadband connection you can still load saved files in the same way.

Method

1. Load your browser but don't connect to the Net. (You might need to select the **Work Offline** option.)
2. Select **Open** from the **File** menu.
3. Browse your directories for the file you saved.
4. Click **OK** to load your file.

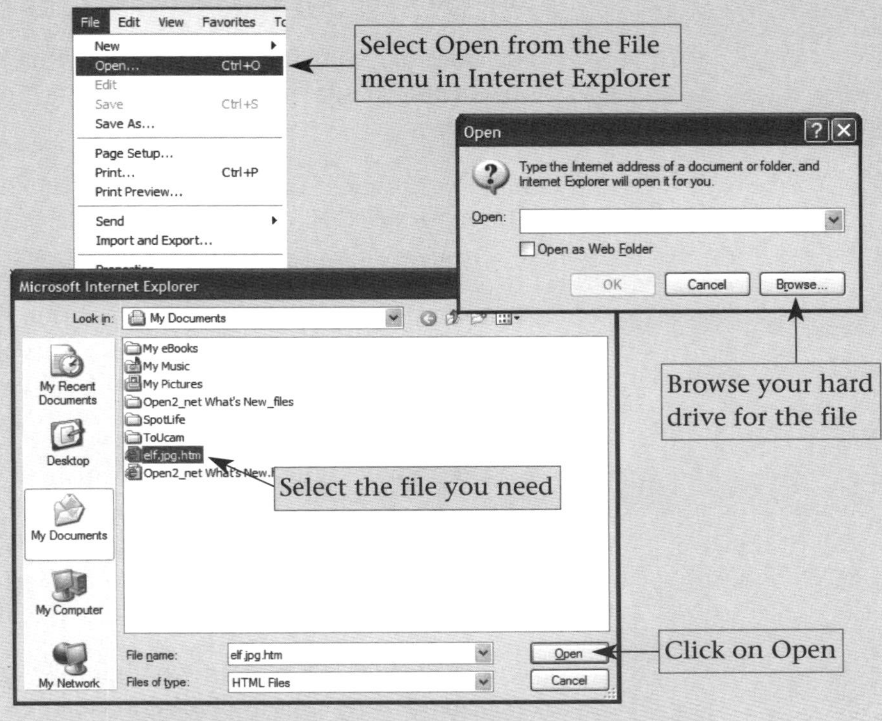

Figure 3.18 Viewing saved information

→ Practise your skills 5

1. Load your browser and connect to your ISP.
2. Go to the Heinemann hotlinks web page for this title and click on ref45a.
3. Select the hyperlink image **mammals** from the **field guides**.
4. Select the hyperlink for **Cheetah** from the list.
5. Save the page as text only.
6. Note down the speed of the cheetah from the information.
7. Select the zoom icon for the **Cheetah**.
8. Save the cheetah image.
9. Save the whole web page.
10. Disconnect and close your browser.
11. Load your saved text file and print out a copy.
12. Load your saved image file and print out a copy.
13. Load your saved web page file and print out a copy.
14. Check the note you made about the cheetah's speed with your printout.

Weblinks:

To access the web site content relevant to this page visit www.heinemann.co.uk/hotlinks

Enter express code 2733P, click GO and then click on the relevant link from the text.

Downloading files

Many of the links on a web page will take you to another web page, either on the same web site or on another web site completely. This is how you can 'surf' from one page to another. Some of the other links on a web page allow you to **download** files or programs to your computer. You need to do this before you can use it or do anything with it.

For example, you may want to download **shareware** or **freeware** from one of the many sites on the Net offering a wide range of these programs.

Some of the most helpful programs you could download are **plug-ins**, which are small programs that work with your browser to give it extra functions.

For example, you may want to add a plug-in which will allow you to play video clips or music, such as Apple's QuickTime for watching videos and animations . . .

. . . or RealAudio© which enables you to play sound effects and music. If a web page has been created using one of these plug-ins, you will need to add that plug-in to your browser to see all the information on the web page. Having downloaded your plug-in, you might then want to download music or video clips to play.

Acrobat Reader is a plug-in which allows anyone to view and print documents in the Adobe Portable Document Format (the file extension is pdf). This is a very popular format for documents, such as reports, forms, manuals and brochures, which you can download and print out, but can't change or edit in any way. When you have the Acrobat Reader installed, you can download any pdf documents from the Net and view them.

Many of these plug-ins are free to download and use.

Task 3.14 Downloading a file

Method

1. Click on the **download** link (usually similar to a hyperlink or a button).
2. Select the **Save** option.
3. Choose where you want to save the file on your hard drive and click on **Save**.

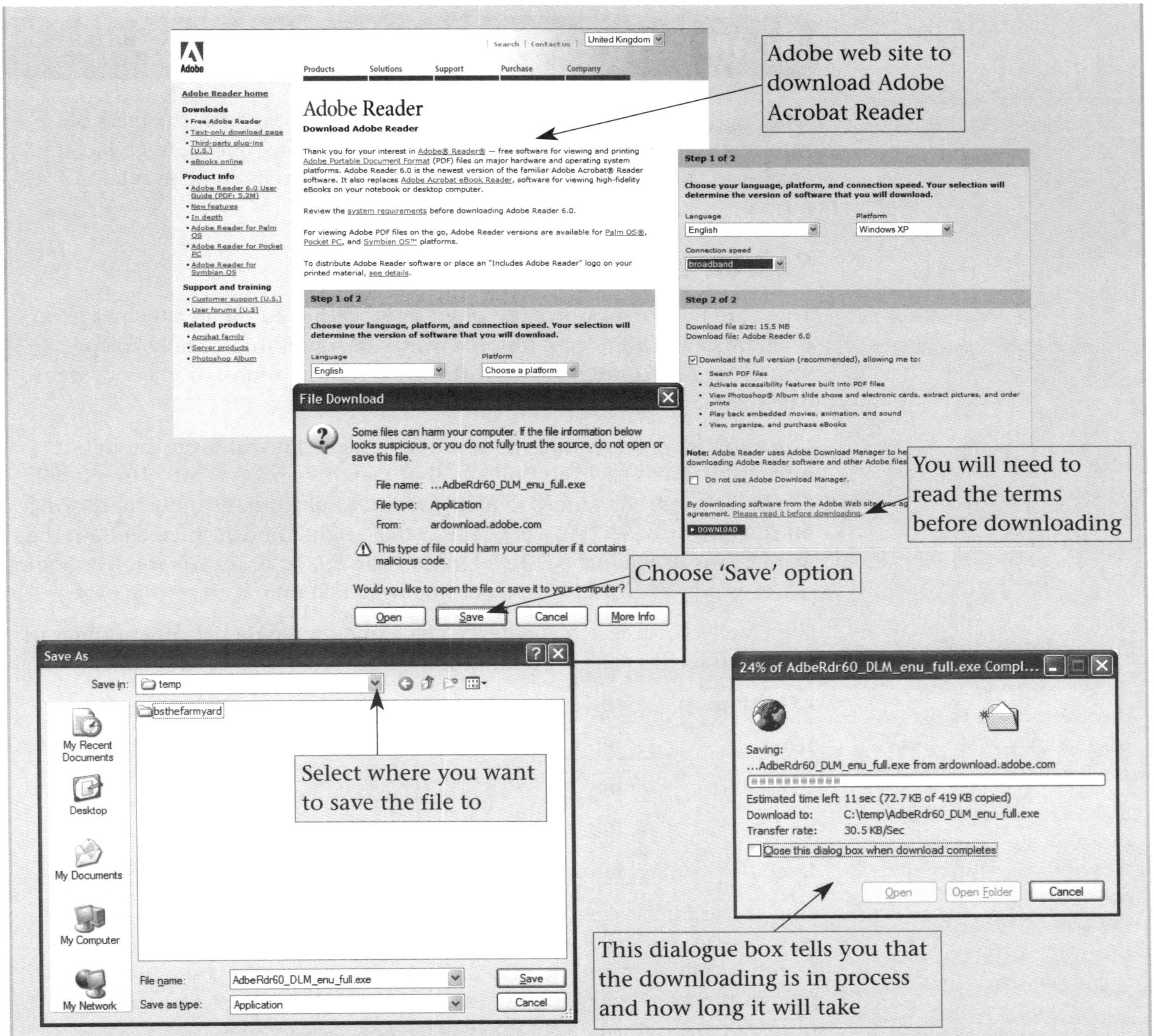

Figure 3.19 Downloading a file

Hint:

Because of the risk of viruses being transmitted from downloaded files, you should always use your virus checker to make sure the file is clear before you open it.

Information

If you select **Open**, it will open the file to view or play straight away (as long as you have the appropriate program loaded onto your computer). This will not download the program or file onto your hard drive.

Information

If you have downloaded a program, such as Acrobat Reader, you will then have to install it onto your computer. If you have downloaded a file, such as a video clip, you will have to load the appropriate application and open the file.

Searching

Finding the particular piece of information you need from the mass of information on the Web might seem a bit daunting, but the Web has the answer in the **search tools** you can use. Search tools come in different forms.

Search engines

These are indexes of web sites, often put together automatically by a program called a spider, a robot, a worm, or something equally creepy sounding! These programs trawl the Web finding information about web pages and adding it to the indexes.

You enter **keywords** into the search engine and it will hunt through its huge lists of web pages to find any that match your keywords. Then it will display the web site names in a list for you to pick from simply by clicking on the link provided. Any page the search engine finds, which contain the word or words you have entered in the search box, is known as a **hit**. Some searches may return thousands of hits which could run to several pages.

Weblinks:

To access the web site content relevant to this page visit www.heinemann.co.uk/hotlinks

Enter express code 2733P, click GO and then click on the relevant link from the text.

Some well known search engines can be found on the Heinemann hotlinks web page for this title. Clicking on the following links will take you to them:

Altavista	ref48a
HotBot	ref48b
Infoseek	ref48c
Excite	ref48d
Lycos	ref48e

One of the advantages of a search engine is that the information in its index is usually up to date. The disadvantage is that keywords entered into the search box may return too many hits, which could take you a long time to plough through. For example, searching for 'mountain pictures' using AltaVista may return 857172 hits.

Using a search engine

To start a simple search you can type in your keyword or keywords and hit the **Search** button. In the following example the keywords are 'mountain pictures'. The number of hits returned is 857172 because both words are searched for separately, so you have matches on both 'mountain' and 'pictures' as well as the whole name. This is obviously not an ideal way to find the information you want, so you need to use more advanced techniques to do your search.

Information

Sometimes clicking on a link in the lists of hits will open up the web page in a new window. You will need to remember to close the window when you have viewed the web site by clicking on the **Close** ☒ button to return to your hit list.

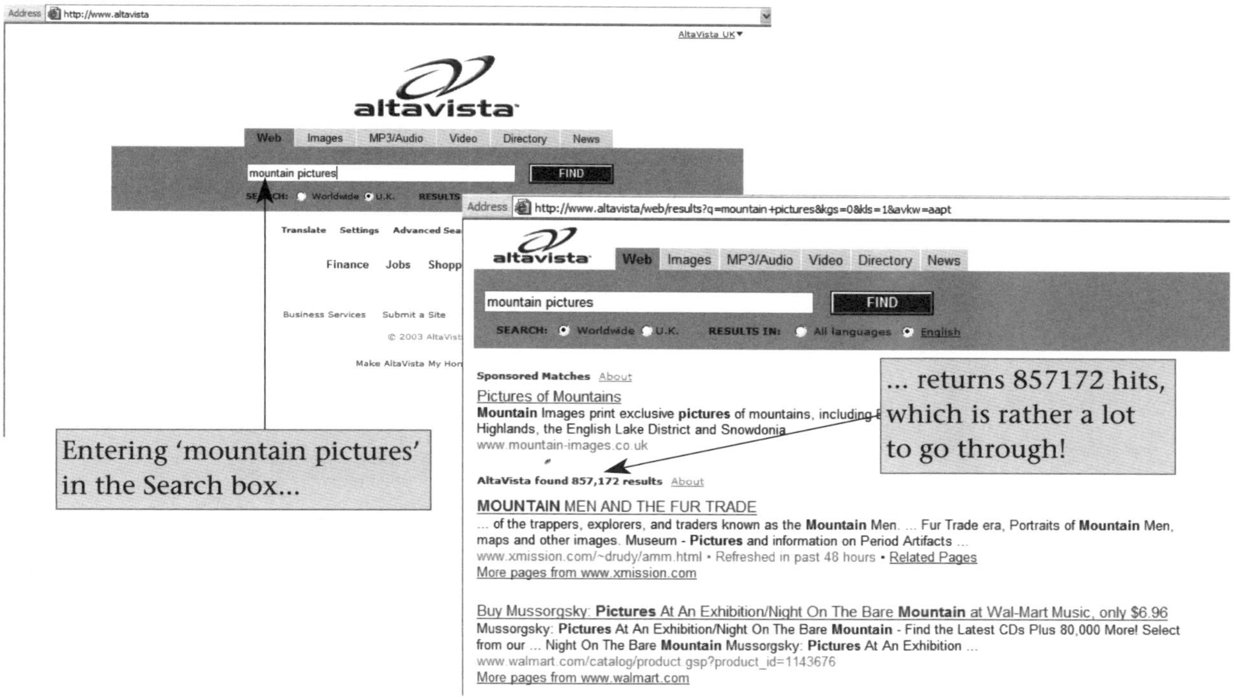

Figure 3.20 Searching the Internet

Ordering your keywords

If you enter your keywords in descending order of importance, for example if you wanted pictures of mountains, type in **pictures mountains**, and the search engine will show the hits for picture sites before the more general sites for mountains. Choosing the top hits from the list will most probably bring up the pages you want.

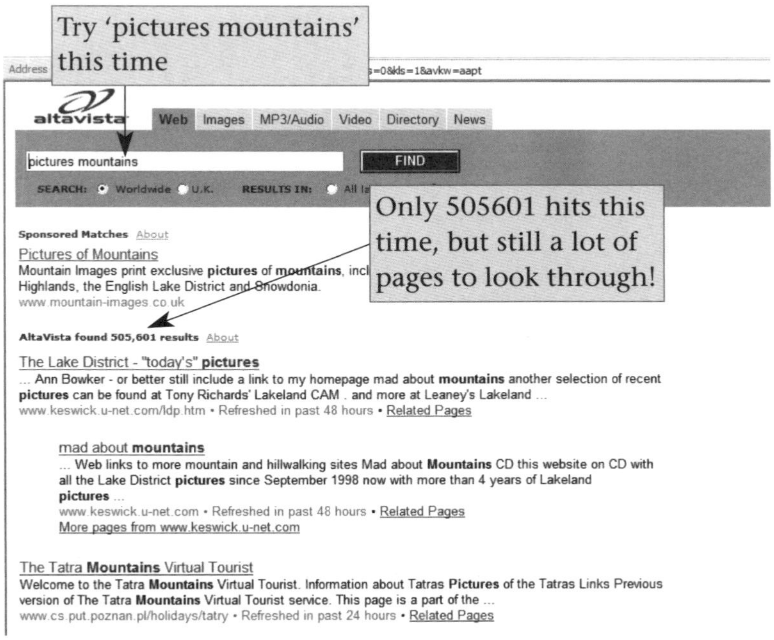

Figure 3.21 The order of keywords can narrow down the search for information

Using "quotation marks"

If you enter your keywords in quote marks, the search engine will look for pages containing *both* the keywords. If we enter the example above as "pictures mountains" we only get 167 hits. These are more likely to be useful pages and there are far fewer of them to look through.

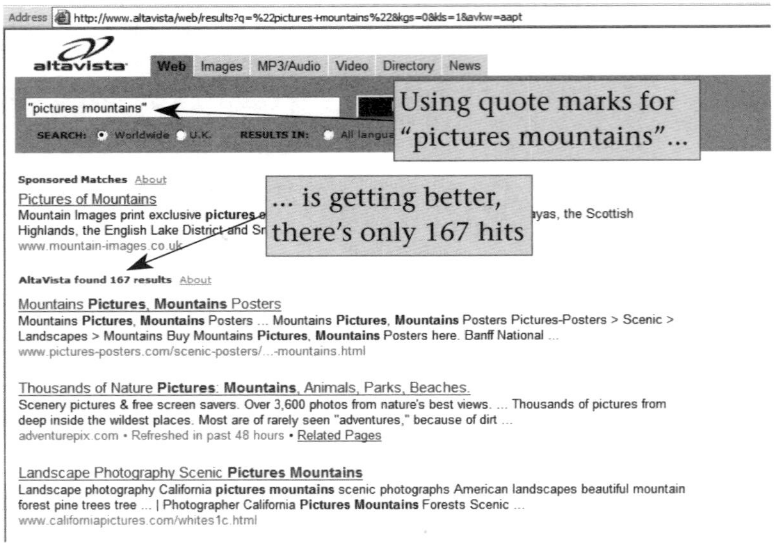

Figure 3.22 Quote marks narrows the search for information even more

Using + and – signs

Placing the + sign between your keywords allows you to be much more specific in your search, as it means that the word which comes after the + sign must be included. So searching for 'diamonds + jewellery' will bring up 12491 hits, and all these sites are likely to be useful. On the other hand, using the – sign tells the search engine to exclude the word which follows. So searching for 'diamonds – jewellery' brings up 65321 hits, but they will just be about the main topic – diamonds, and not about jewellery.

> **Hint:**
>
> Using **AND** or **NOT** (or AND NOT) instead of the + and – signs will have the same effect in your search.

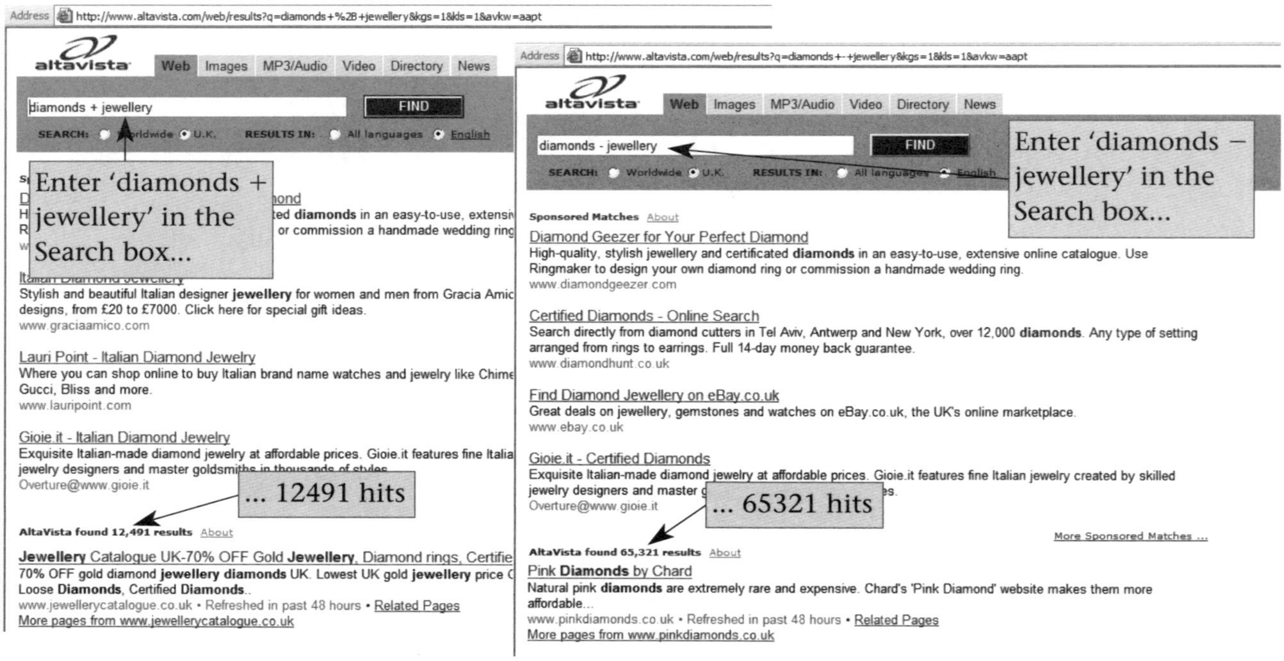

Figure 3.23 Using + and – to search for information

Hint:

Search engines are not usually case sensitive, i.e. it doesn't matter if you type them in capital or lower case letters, but it is important that you spell the words correctly, otherwise you might end up with no hits at all.

Using a question

With most search engines you cannot just type in your question and find the answer straight away. There is one exception. You can **Ask Jeeves** at www.ask.co.uk. Simply type in your question/search, using keywords or phrases, such as 'What is the highest mountain?', and Ask Jeeves will present you with a set of relevant results and also make suggestions of alternative searches that might be relevant to your query. It will also give you the best result for what you're searching for.

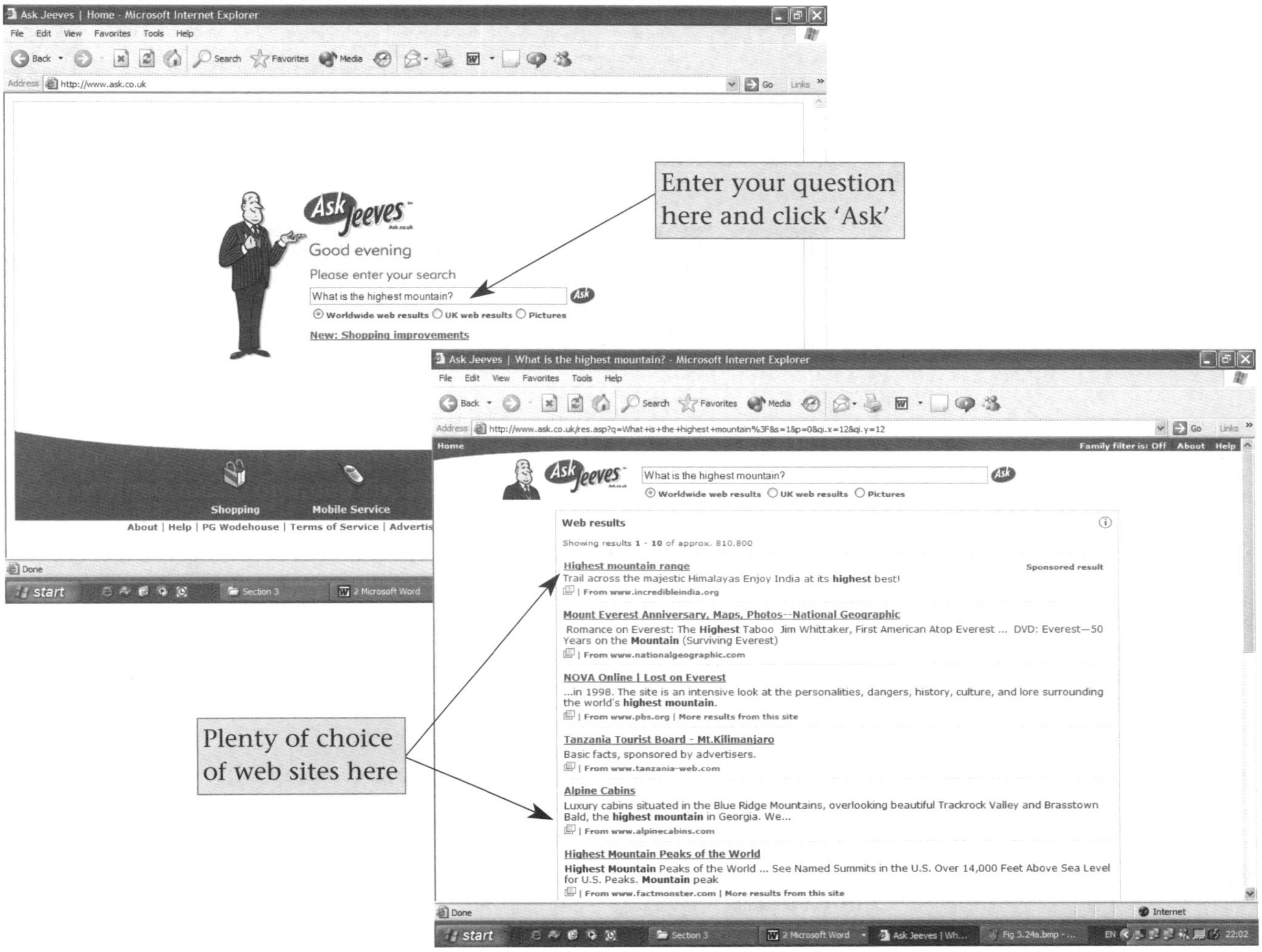

Figure 3.24 Asking a question to find what you are looking for on the Internet

Directories

Directories have their data sorted into categories, such as Society and Culture or Computers and the Internet. They are organised in a similar way to your folders on your hard drive. Click on a category and you will get another level listing related topics about the main category. By continuing to select sub-categories, you will eventually reach the subject you want to find out about. You can see how this works by following the links to find out about mountains, starting at the Yahoo Homepage.

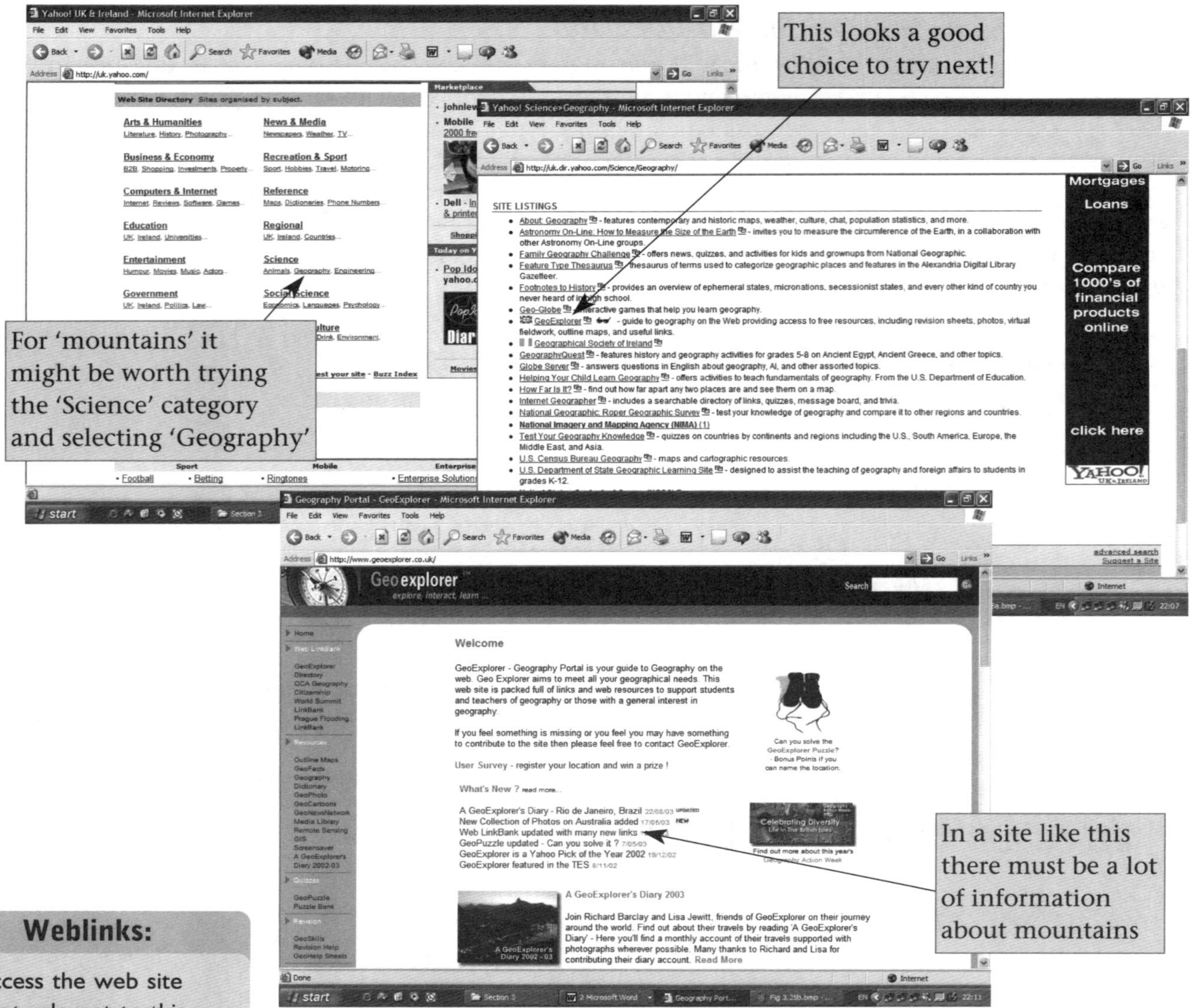

Figure 3.25 Searching through directories

Some well known directories can be found on the Heinemann hotlinks web page for this title. Clicking on the following links will take you to them:

Google	ref52a
Looksmart	ref52b
Yahoo!	ref52c
UK Online	ref52d

Information

Increasingly the distinction between pure search engines and directories is becoming blurred as the top-of-the-range search engines are offering directories and vice versa.

As each of these search tools serves a different purpose, you will find that one may be useful for one type of search you need to do, while another may be the best option for another topic you want to find out about. It's always best to have a selection of different search tools to choose from.

Weblinks:

To access the web site content relevant to this page visit www.heinemann.co.uk/hotlinks

Enter express code 2733P, click GO and then click on the relevant link from the text.

Hint:

You can bookmark or add these search tool URLs to your **Favorites**. You could set up a search tool folder in your Favorites and keep all the ones you like to use together where you can load them with just a single click. The choice of search tool you use most often will be a matter of personal taste.

Meta searches

Even using the tips for advanced searching, you could still find that you need to work through several search engines to locate a piece of information that is particularly hard to find. Although a **meta search site** looks like any other search site, it is different in that it submits your keywords to multiple search engines at the same time and produces just one list of hits for you to choose from. This can save you quite a lot of time when searching and following links to find the web page you want.

Weblinks:

To access the web site content relevant to this page visit www.heinemann.co.uk/hotlinks

Enter express code 2733P, click GO and then click on the relevant link from the text.

Some well known meta search sites can be found on the Heinemann hotlinks web page for this title. Clicking on the following links will take you to them:

MetaCrawler ref53a

Dogpile ref53b

Copernic ref53c

→ Practise your skills 6

1 You are going to test five search engines or directories. Four are listed below and you must add one other of your own. To get to them visit the Heinemann hotlinks web page for this title and click on the following links:

Yahoo ref53d
Lycos ref53e
Ask Jeeves ref53f
AltaVista ref53g

Using each of the search engines or directories find the following information:

- What is the Mariana Trench?
- Directions and map to Jodrell Bank Planetarium.
- What is the population of the UK?
- What is the current line up of the Manchester United football team?

2 Note down the number of 'hits' for each search engine or directory, and print out a copy of your search results.

Printing web pages

Having successfully found the web page with the information you need, you might want to print it out. You might want just the picture or a bit of the text, or maybe the whole page. However, if you click on the Internet Explorer **Print** button, you may get more than you bargained for – pages and pages of print!

Task 3.15 Setting up the printer

Method

1 Select **Page Setup** from the **File** menu.
2 Change the settings for paper size, orientation, etc. as you require.
3 Click on **OK**.

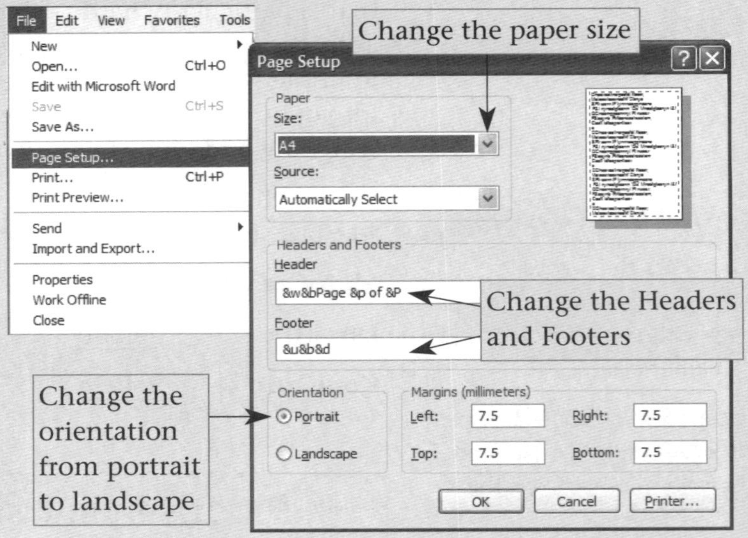

Figure 3.26 Setting up to print

Task 3.16 Printing a web page

Method

1 Select **Print** from the **File** menu.
2 The **Print** dialogue box will open. If you have more than one printer available, select the printer you want to use.
3 Under the **General** tab, choose the appropriate options for printing.
4 If the web page is divided into frames, click on the **Options** tab and select the appropriate frame you want in the **Print Frames** section.
5 Click on **Apply**, and then on **Print**.

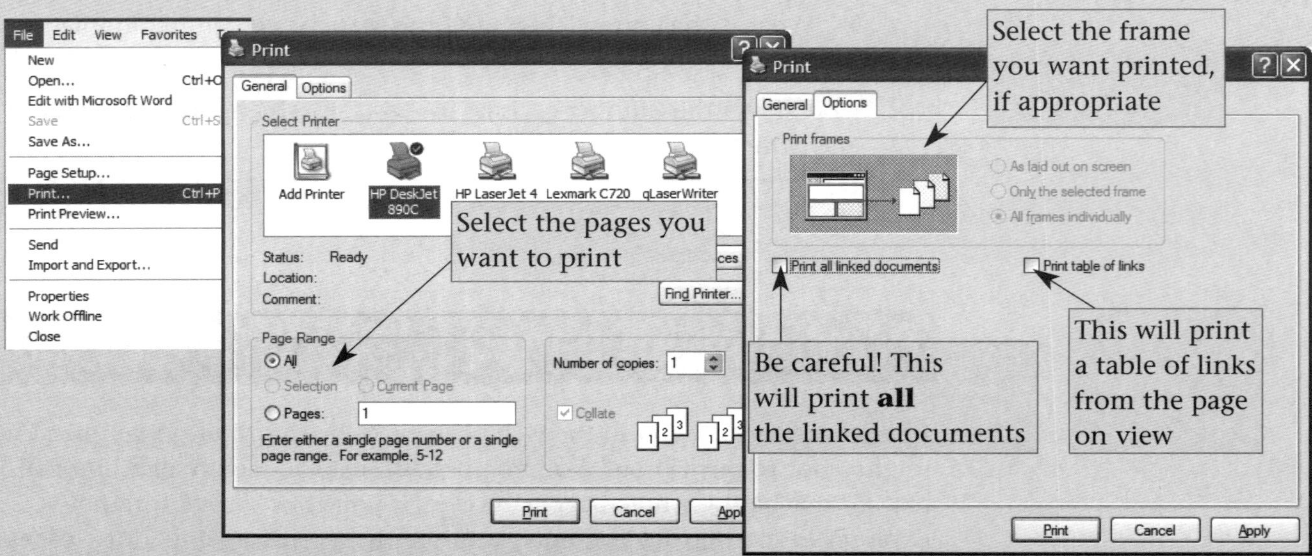

Figure 3.27 Printing a web page

Task 3.17 Printing text

This isn't quite so easy, as you will need to select the text, copy it to the clipboard and paste it into a word processing application, such as Word, before printing it out.

Method

1. Select the text on the web page that you want to print.
2. Copy the selection (use **Ctrl + C** or **Copy** from the **Edit** menu).
3. Open your word processing program.
4. Paste the selection into your open document (use **Ctrl + V** or **Paste** from the **Edit** menu).
5. Reformat the text if necessary.
6. Print out the document.

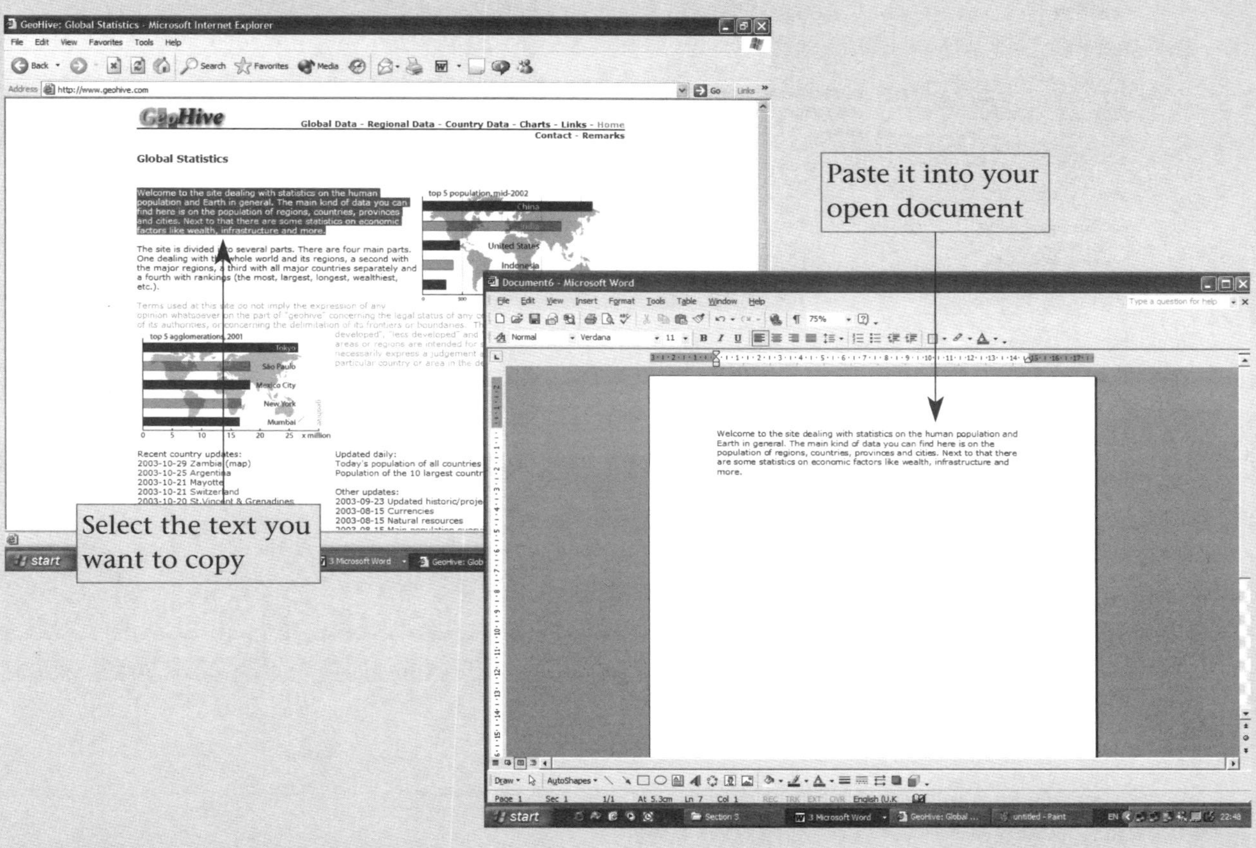

Figure 3.28 Printing text from a web page

Hint:

If you select text and click on the **Print** button on Internet Explorer's toolbar, you will get a printout of the whole web page.

Information

When you have pasted and formatted the text in your word processing program, you can save it to your hard drive or floppy disk just like any other word processed file.

Task 3.18 Printing pictures

This is very similar to printing a selection of text.

Method

1. Right mouse click on your chosen picture.
2. Select **Copy** from the pop-up menu.
3. Open your image editing program, **Paint** for example.
4. **Paste** the image into the open document.
5. Click on **Print**.

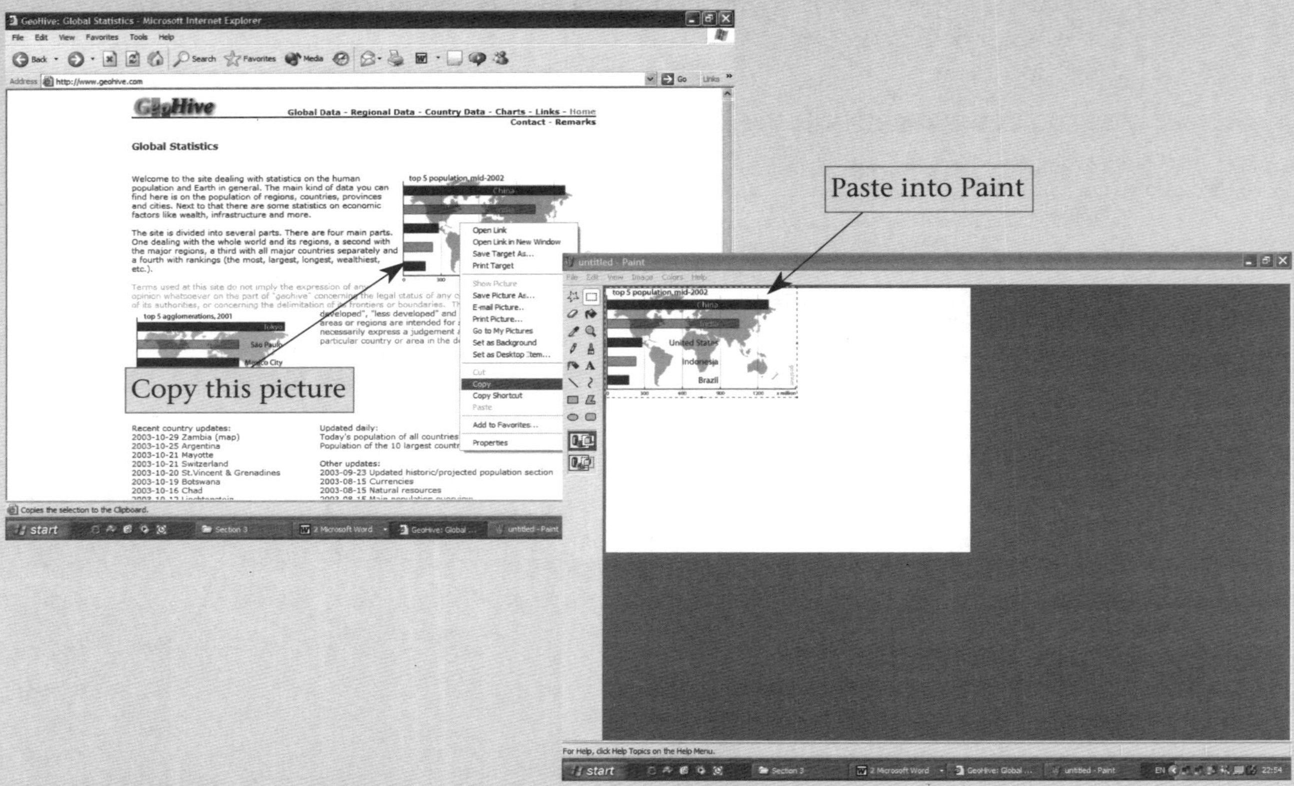

Figure 3.29 Printing a picture from a web page

Hint:

If you select **Print Target** from the pop-up menu, you will find that you are printing a copy of the web page that you would be taken to if you clicked on the picture.

Information

You can also paste your image into a word processing document. This would be useful if you were writing a report or producing a leaflet, for example, and wanted the image to illustrate your point.

→ Practise your skills 7

It is said that you can find out about anything on the Internet if you have the time and patience, but is that really true? In this exercise you are going to use the Web to find out the answers to your own Internet Quiz.

1. Choose a topic for your quiz. This could be an area that interests you or it may be geographical, historical, scientific or another factually based subject.
2. Use a word processing program to enter the ten questions you would use for your quiz.
3. Using the Internet, search for and identify the answers you need using a variety of search methods and enter the URLs onto your question sheet.
4. Save the web pages with the answers as text-only files and as whole web page files. Print out copies.
5. Add the web pages with the answers to your Favorites folder.
6. Organise your Favorites folder by creating a new folder called 'Internet Quiz', and move all the web page addresses with the answers to this folder.
7. Open your History folder and select the date when you completed this exercise. Take a screen shot and print out a copy.

→ Check your knowledge

1. How can you tell if an image or text on a web page is a hyperlink?
2. What is the Favorites folder?
3. What are Bookmarks?
4. How would you load a web page if you knew the URL?
5. How would you change the length of time your web pages stay in your History folder?
6. Why do you need to be careful when downloading files from the Internet?
7. What is the main difference between a search engine and a directory?
8. What are the advanced techniques for entering keywords in a search engine?
9. What is a meta search site?
10. If you wanted to just print the text from a web page, why would you not click on the **Print** button on the toolbar?

Section 4 Keeping in touch

You will learn to

- Identify software suitable for using e-mail
- Use e-mail software and identify features of e-mail
  - ☐ create e-mail messages
  - ☐ send e-mail messages
  - ☐ retrieve e-mail messages
  - ☐ read e-mail messages
  - ☐ delete e-mail messages
  - ☐ forward e-mail messages
  - ☐ open attached files
  - ☐ attach files to e-mail messages
  - ☐ save and print e-mail messages
  - ☐ use an e-mail file management system
  - ☐ shut down an e-mail program
- Identify the uses of e-mail
- Identify the advantages of using e-mail

Introduction: electronic mail

One of the quickest ways of communicating with others on a network is to use **electronic mail**, or **e-mail** as it is usually called. This is a method of sending letters, memos, pictures and sounds from one computer to another. If you are at home, you may use a modem to connect to your phone line so that you can send e-mails to anywhere in the world and receive e-mails in reply. This is often quicker than 'snail mail' (the name sometimes used for the postal system) and, usually, just for the cost of a local phone call.

To send and receive e-mails you will need some basic equipment: a computer, a modem, an e-mail program (such as Outlook Express), and an account with an Internet Service Provider to access the Internet. The e-mail system is very much like a postal service. You send e-mails through your ISP's post office to the post offices of your recipients' ISPs, where the messages wait until they next log on to their ISPs.

If you are on a network, you will be able to send messages to other people in your organisation as well as sending them to people outside the network through a phone line, ISDN (Integrated Services Digital Network) connection, or a broadband connection. Whether you are sending or receiving e-mails internally or externally you will need to have e-mail software, such as Microsoft **Outlook Express**, installed on your computer or network. There are many e-mail programs available, most of which perform similar tasks of sending and receiving e-mail messages, although they might look different and some may have more advanced features than

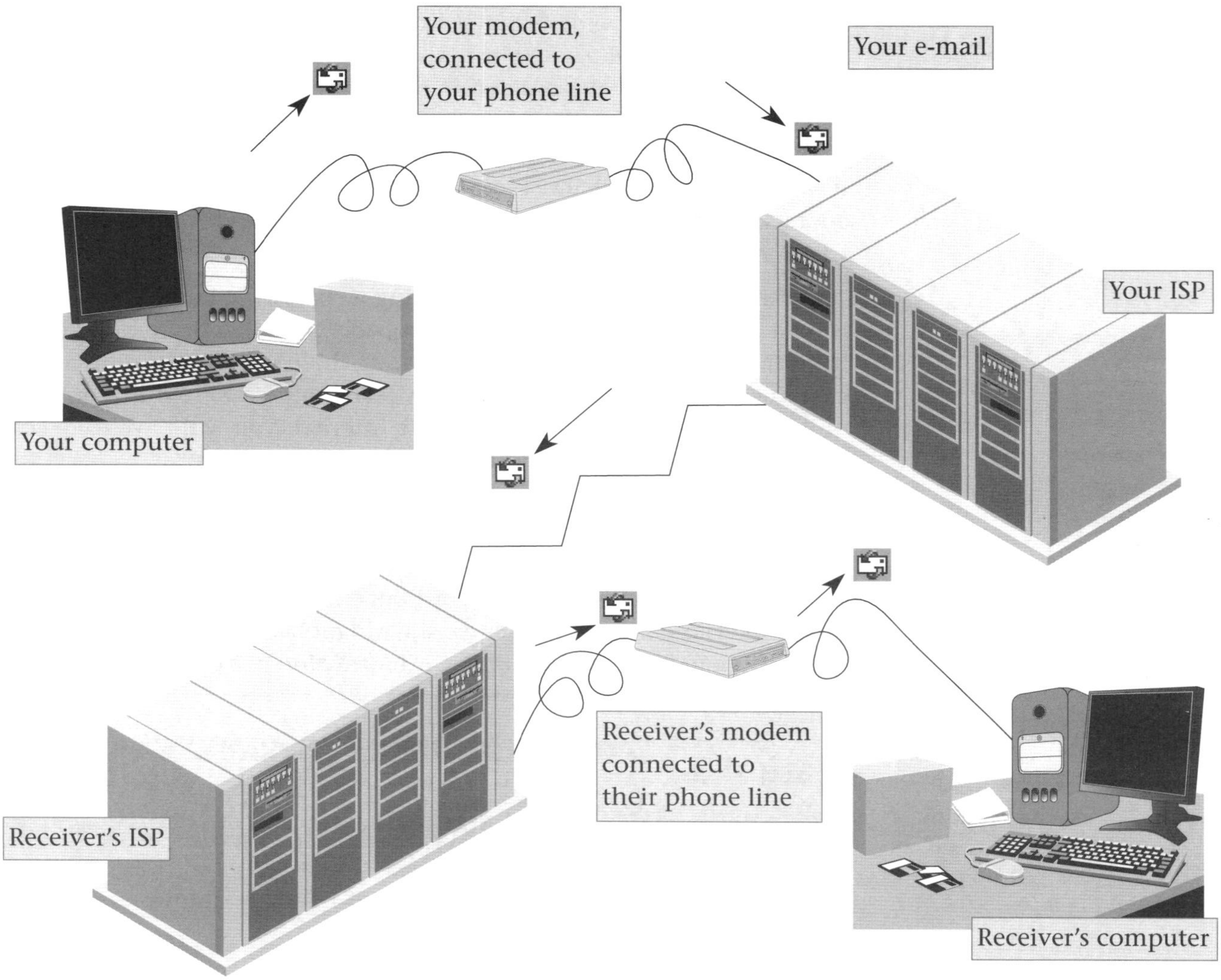

Figure 4.1 The journey an e-mail makes from sender to receiver

others. Netscape Mail and Eudora are among some of the other popular e-mail programs. Most of the software provided by ISPs will have e-mail programs included.

Using e-mail software

Web-based e-mail

With Outlook Express or another e-mail program loaded onto your computer, you can compose your e-mails when you are offline and just connect to the Net to send (and check) your mail. This saves considerable money in call charges but can be a problem if you need to check your mail when you are away from home. You can certainly connect to your ISP wherever you may be, but can you imagine the cost of the call if you were sunning yourself on a tropical beach? This is when web-based e-mail can be a good option. Instead of using a dedicated e-mail program, you can create a free account with a web-based e-mail service such as Hotmail or Excite mail.

You will have a new e-mail address which will be similar to josie@hotmail.com. You can read and write your e-mails by logging on to your e-mail service and entering your personal username and password. It doesn't matter where you are in the world, you can still pick up your mail and reply using any of the cyber cafés or hotel Internet facilities anywhere in the world. It can be very useful to have both an e-mail facility provided by your ISP and a web-based e-mail address, but you will have to make sure that people know which one to use and when to use it if you are going away.

There are certain disadvantages to using web-based e-mail. You still need a way of connecting to the Internet, probably provided by an ISP. You have to be online to read and write your e-mails, which could mount up to quite a cost in call charges, and you can only read your e-mails while you are online. Once you disconnect from the Internet, you will have to re-connect if you need to check the details of a message's contents.

Weblinks:

To access the web site content relevant to this page visit www.heinemann.co.uk/hotlinks

Enter express code 2733P, click GO and then click on the relevant link from the text.

Information

Many ISPs will allow you to set up your e-mail program to access your Hotmail account. Your ISP's web site will probably have the details of how to go about it, or you may find the information in a computer magazine.

Task 4.1 Creating a web-based e-mail account (using Hotmail for this example)

The following shows you how to create an e-mail account.

Method

1. Connect to the Internet.
2. Load the web page for Hotmail. A link for this site can be found on the Heinemann hotlinks web page for this title (ref60a).
3. Complete the form with your details.
4. **Sign in**.

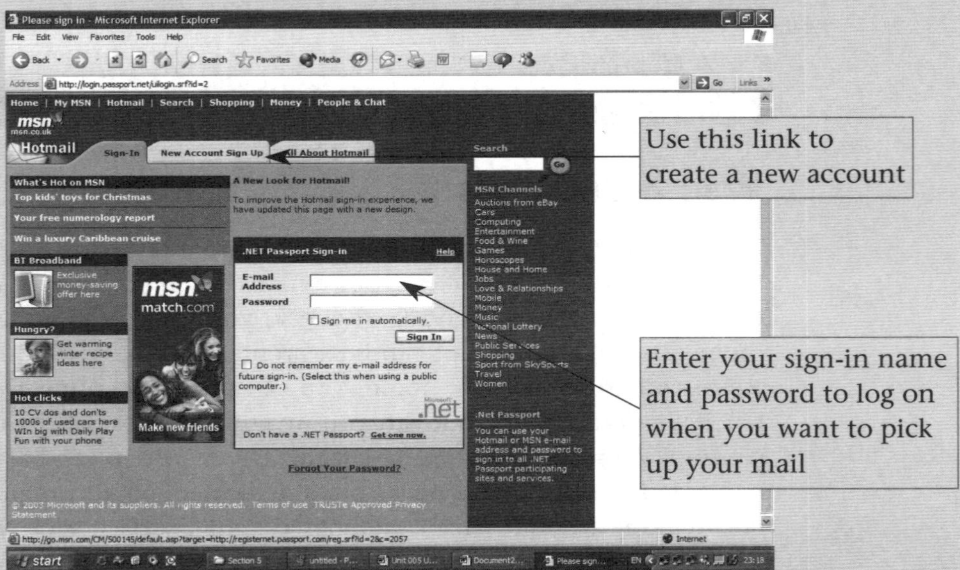

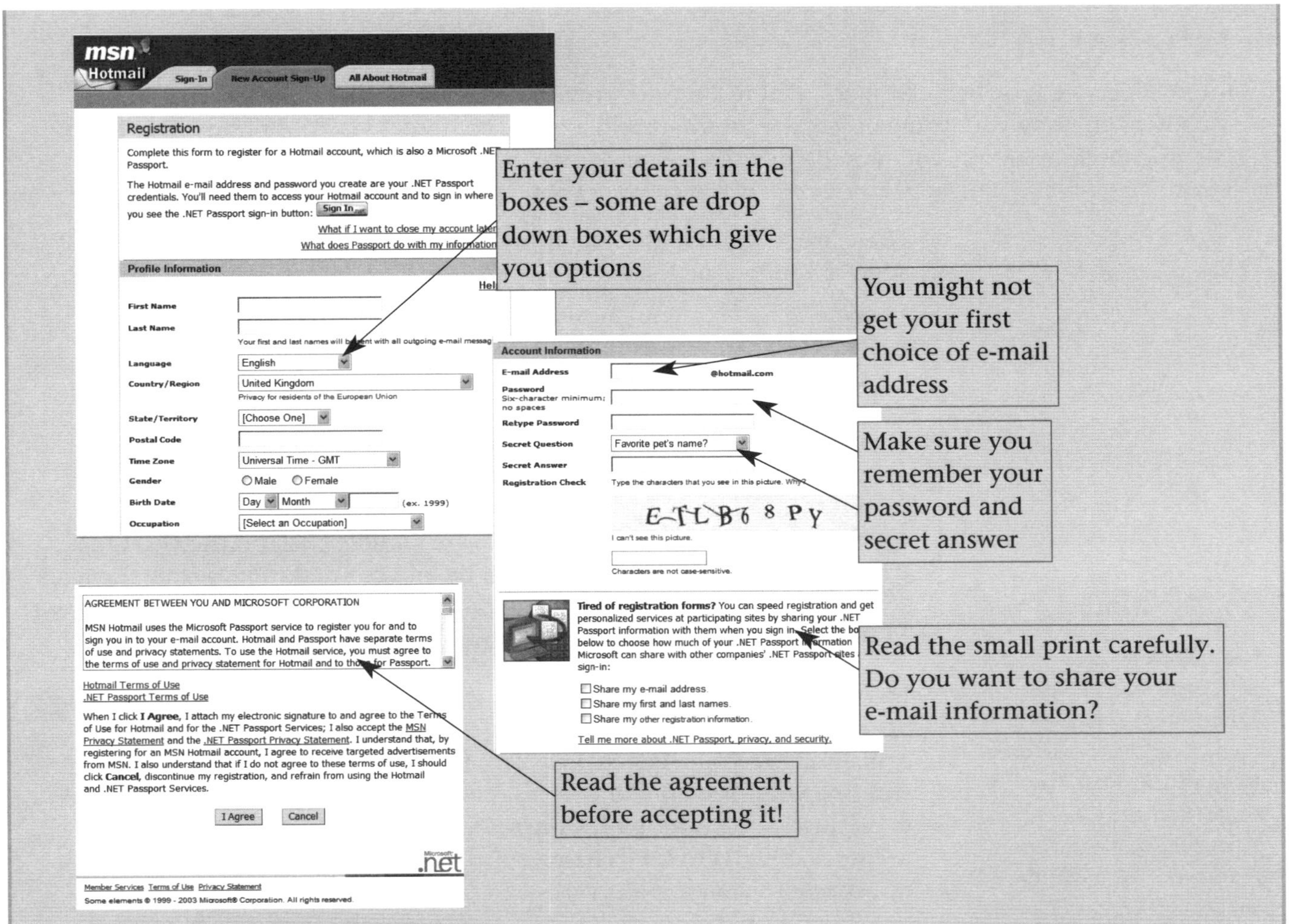

Figure 4.2 Creating a web-based e-mail account

Now you can collect your e-mail wherever you are.

Sending e-mails

To send an e-mail to someone, you will need to know his or her e-mail address. This is a unique address that will look something like the one shown below:

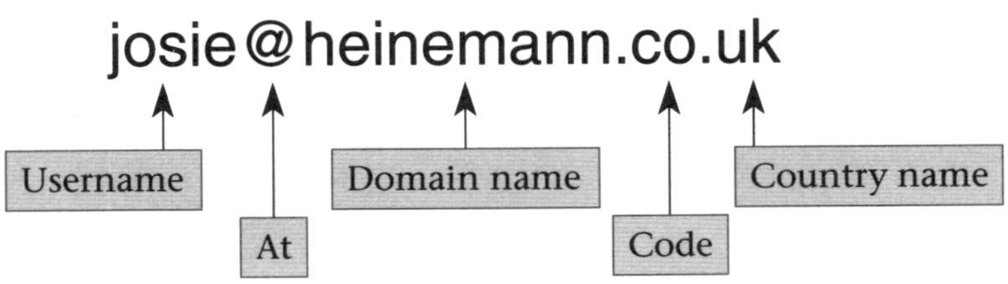

- **Username** The name or nickname of the person.
- **Domain name** The unique address of the computer – this has three main sections that tell you where the computer is.
  - ☐ **heinemann** the organisation where the user works or the **Internet Service Provider's** name.
  - ☐ **co** this tells you the type of organisation.
  - ☐ **uk** this tells you the country.

Information

Internet Service Providers (ISPs) and Online Services provide a gateway to the Internet. This would usually be the way you would access the Internet from a home computer via your phone line. Many ISPs and Online Services will provide this service for a small monthly fee.

There are several types of organisations and you can tell from the e-mail address which type it is:

- **ac** an academic organisation
- **co** or **com** a commercial organisation
- **edu** an educational institution
- **gov** a government body
- **net** an organisation involved in running the Net
- **org** a non-profit-making organisation

To start your **e-mail** software, double click on the **Outlook Express** icon, which will be on your desktop, or click the icon on the taskbar or in the programs menu (if you have a different e-mail package, you will need to open this program instead).

Hint:

The following screen shots use **Outlook Express**. Although the windows might look slightly different if you're using another e-mail package, the procedures for using your system will be much the same.

You will find a window similar to the one shown here.

The **Dial-up Connection** box will open. You now have the choice of connecting to your service provider by entering your password and username as required and clicking on **Connect**, or by selecting **Work Offline** you can compose your e-mails without running up call charges.

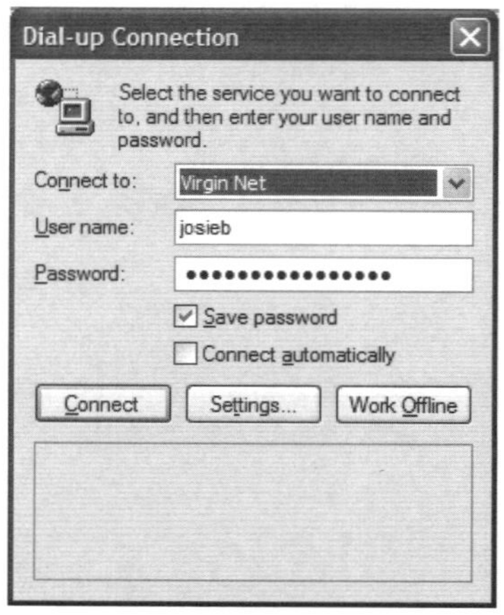

Figure 4.3 Connecting to an ISP

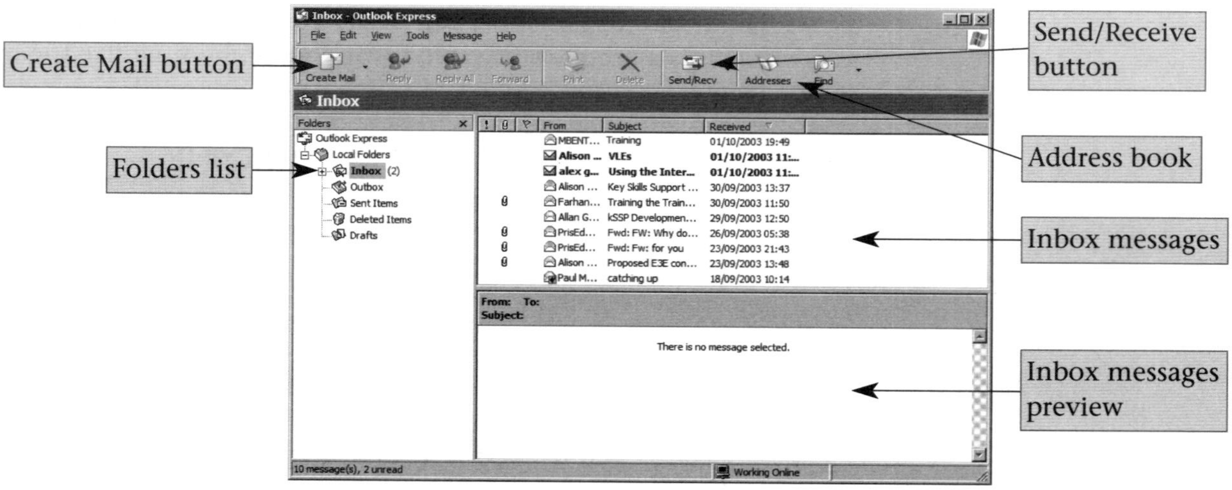

Figure 4.4 An e-mail window

The Outlook Express toolbar

The toolbar provides access to some of the main functions, including sending and receiving e-mails, printing them and deleting messages.

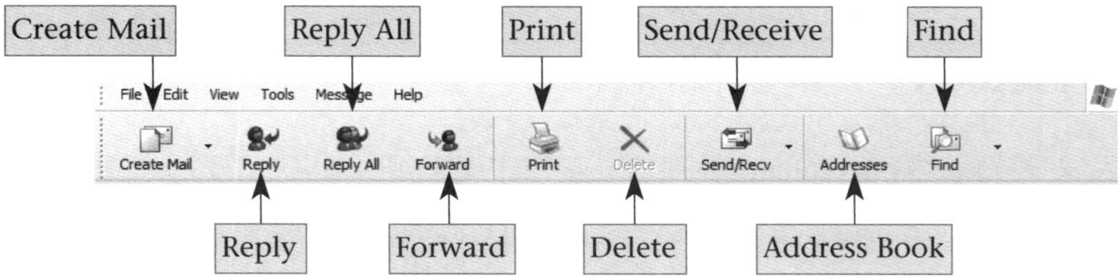

Figure 4.5 The toolbar

- **Create mail** This opens a blank e-mail message window.
- **Reply** Click on this to reply to any selected message in your Inbox. A new message window opens with the address already entered in the **To:** box. You can choose to have the message copied in your reply.
- **Reply All** You can reply to a message and send that reply to all the others who have received the same message.
- **Forward** This button allows you to forward any message to someone else by filling in the appropriate address in the **To:** box.
- **Print** If you want a copy of your e-mail, click on this button.
- **Delete** You can tidy up your folders by deleting any selected messages you no longer want.
- **Send/Recv** This will send any messages in your **Outbox** and check for new mail (assuming you're online).
- **Addresses** To open your address book, use this button.
- **Find** This button will open a dialogue box to allow you to search for a message.

In the folders list you will have:

- **Inbox** This is where the messages you receive are stored.
- **Outbox** This is where messages you are sending are stored.
- **Sent Items** This folder stores the messages you have sent.
- **Deleted Items** This is where any messages you have deleted are stored.
- **Drafts** This is where messages you are still working on are stored.

If you click on a folder, it will show you all the messages stored inside it.

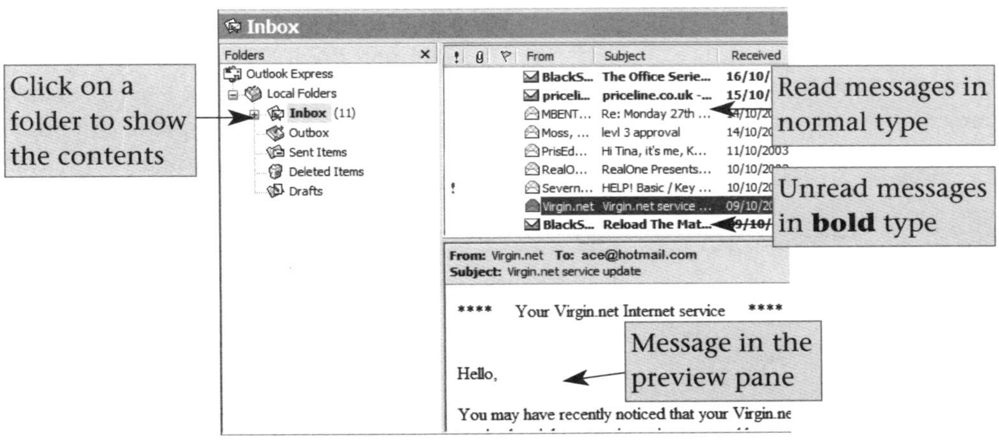

Figure 4.6 E-mail messages stored in a folder

Task 4.2 Sending an e-mail

The following is the procedure for sending an e-mail.

Method

1. Click on the **Create Mail** button 

2. The **New Message** window will appear.
3. Click in the **To:** box, and type in the e-mail address of the person you are sending the message to.
4. Click in the **Subject:** box, and type in a word or short sentence to indicate what the message is about.
5. Click in the message section underneath, and type in your message.
6. Click on the **Send** button 

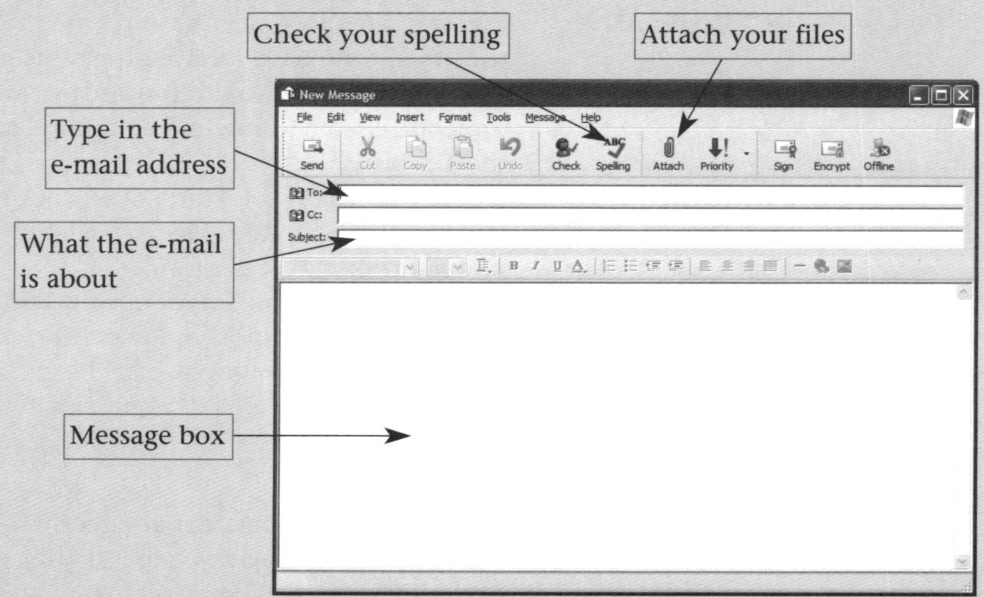

Figure 4.7 Sending an e-mail

Remember:

Check your typing carefully – make sure you haven't left any spaces in the address or left out any of the full stops.

Hint:

You can use the spellchecking button  to check that you haven't made any spelling errors.

If you are using an internal network, your message will be sent straight away. This will also happen if your network has a permanent connection to the phone system or to an ISDN line. A copy of the message will be placed in your **Sent Items** folder. If you have prepared your message **offline** (not connected) your message will be place in your **Outbox** folder. It will remain there until you connect to your ISP and click on the **Send and Receive All** button.

Information

When you click on the **Send/Receive All** button, or when you first log on to your ISP, your e-mail program will usually check for and download any mail which is waiting for you on your ISP server.

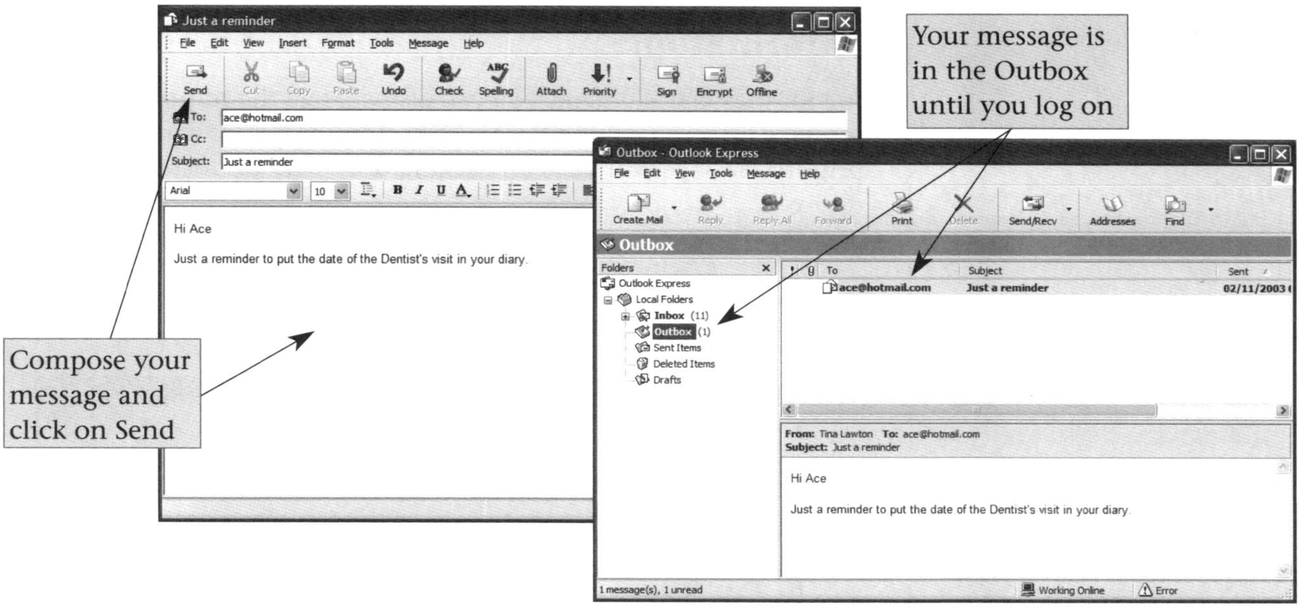

Figure 4.8 An e-mail message held in the Outbox

Information

You can change the send options by choosing the **Options** item from the **Tools** menu. Using the **Send** tab in the dialogue box you can select or de-select items by clicking in the appropriate boxes. For example, you may not want a copy of your message placed in your **Sent Items** folder so you would uncheck the box next to the 'Save copy of sent messages in the 'Sent Items' folder'.

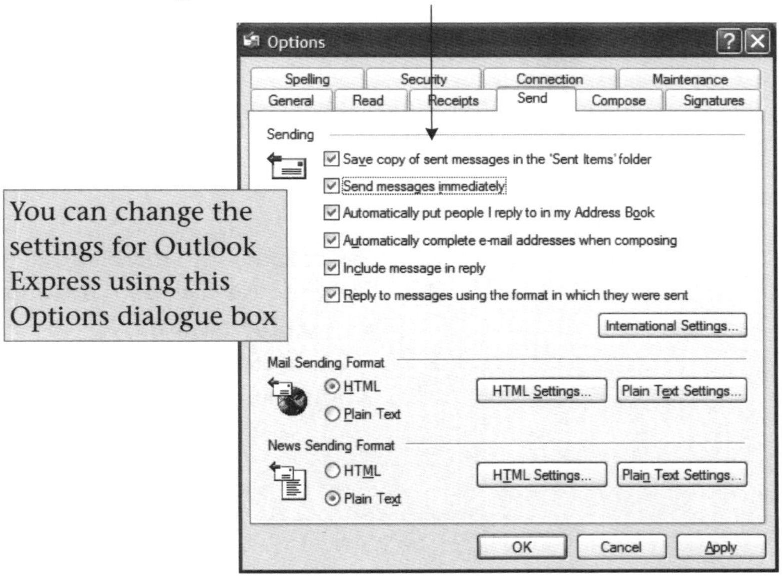

Figure 4.9 Changing the send options

Hint:

If you make changes to your **Options** in Outlook Express but decide that you didn't want to '**Apply**' the changes, you can always click on the **Cancel** button, which will leave the settings as they were before you began.

Information

If your message is urgent, you can also change the priority of the message by selecting the **Priority** button on the toolbar. A high priority message will have an exclamation mark against it when it is received.

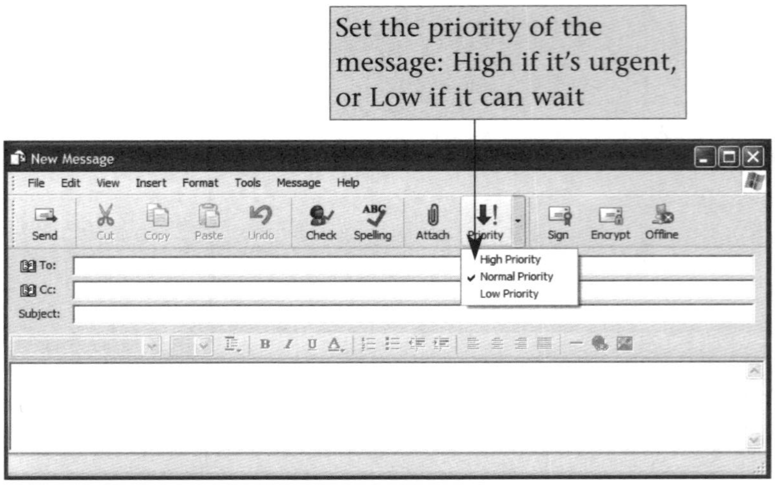

Figure 4.10 Changing the priority of a message

> **Remember:**
>
> If you forget to disconnect from your ISP you could end up with a large phone bill! It's worth getting into the habit of disconnecting every time you close your e-mail program or browser.

When you have sent your e-mail, you will need to close your e-mail program and disconnect from your ISP.

Task 4.3 Closing your e-mail program and disconnecting

Method

1 Select **Exit** from the **File** menu.

2 Right mouse click on the **Connected**  icon on the taskbar.

3 Select **Disconnect** from the pop-up menu which appears.

Figure 4.11 Select Exit

Figure 4.12 Select Disconnect

→ Practise your skills 1

1 Open your e-mail program.
2 Start a new message.
3 Enter the e-mail address of someone you know or your tutor.
4 Enter 'Sending e-mail' in the **Subject** box.
5 Type in this message: 'This is to let you know that I'm sending you an e-mail message to say Hello. Please will you let me know that it has reached you safely.'
6 **Send** the message. (If you are working offline you will need to connect to your ISP.)
7 Close your e-mail program.

Task 4.4 Sending a message to several people

You can send one message to several people at the same time by entering all the e-mail addresses in the **To:** box.

Method

1 Click on the **Create Mail** button.
2 In the **To:** box, enter the e-mail addresses of the people to whom you want to send the e-mail, separated by a comma or a semi-colon (;).

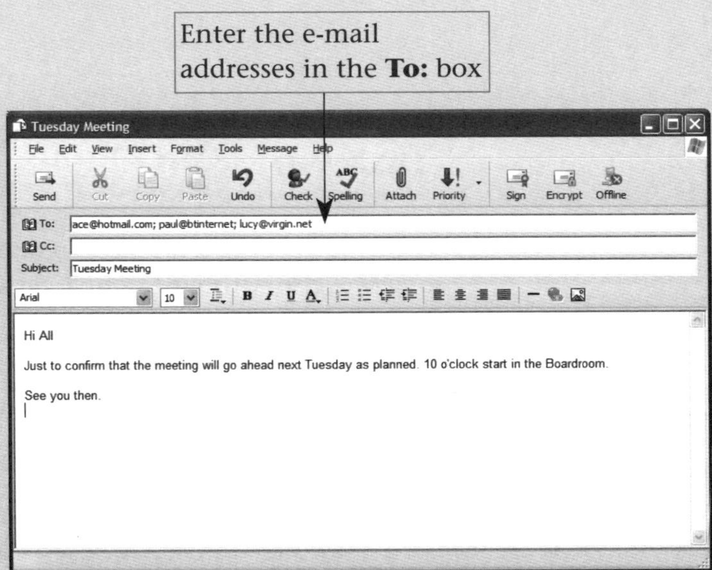

Figure 4.13 Sending an e-mail to several people

3 Complete and send your message in the normal way.

Task 4.5 Sending a copy of a message

If you want to send a copy of your e-mail to someone else, you can use the **Cc:** box to enter the appropriate e-mail address.

Method

1. Click on the **Create Mail** button.
2. Enter the e-mail address of the person to whom you are sending the message in the **To:** box.
3. Click in the **Cc:** box and enter the e-mail address of the person to whom you are sending a copy of the message.
4. Complete and send your message in the normal way.

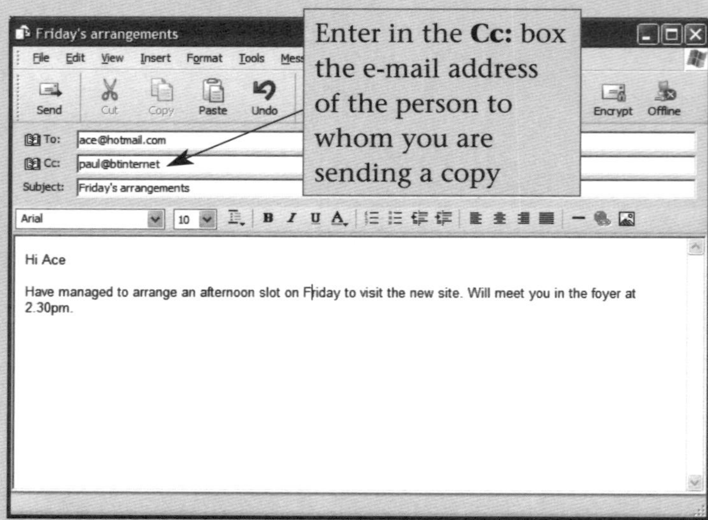

Figure 4.14 Sending a copy of an e-mail

Task 4.6 Sending a blind carbon copy

If you are sending a message to one person, but want to send a copy to someone else without the first person knowing, you can use the **Blind Carbon Copy, Bcc:** option.

Method

1. Click on the **Create Mail** button.
2. Enter the e-mail address of the person to whom you are sending the message in the **To:** box.
3. Select **All Headers** from the **View** menu. A new box will appear below the Cc: box.
4. Click in the **Bcc:** box and enter the e-mail address of the person to whom you are sending a copy of the message.
5. Complete and send your message in the normal way.

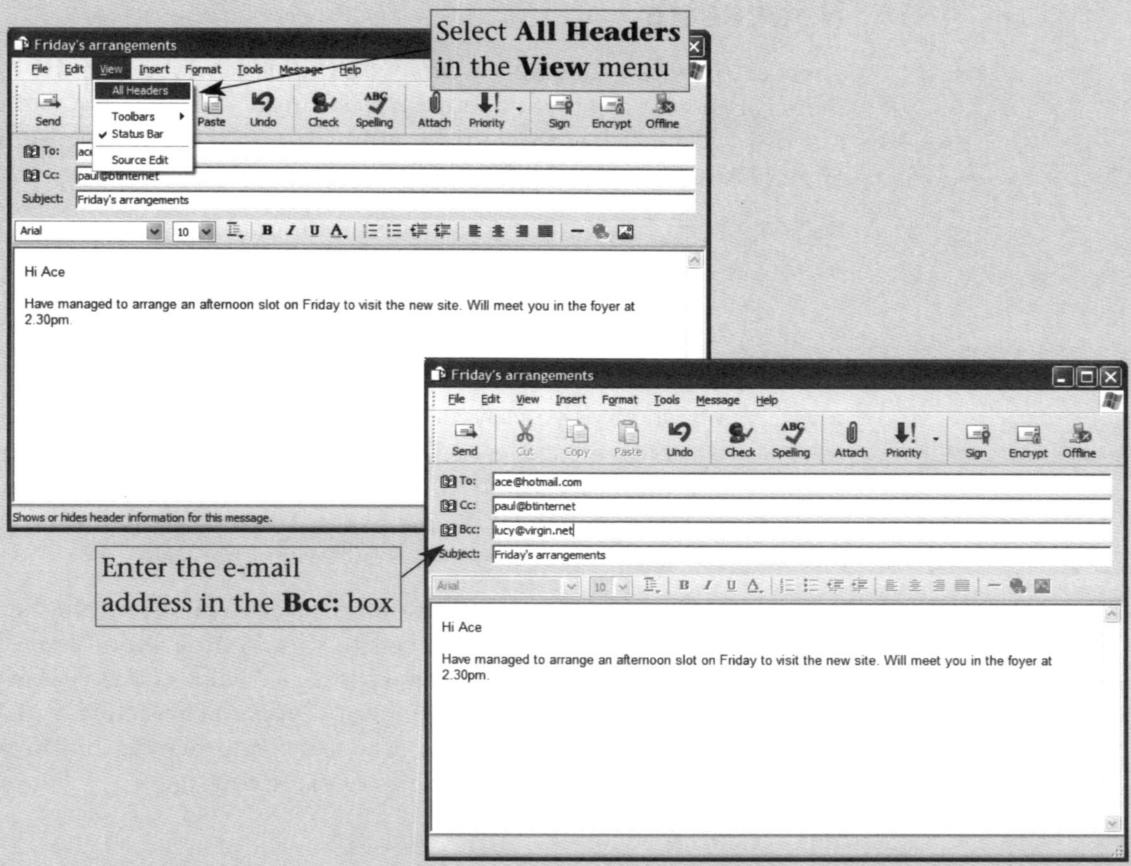

Figure 4.15 Sending a blind carbon copy of an e-mail message

→ Practise your skills 2

1. Open your e-mail program.
2. Start a new message.
3. Enter the e-mail address of someone you know or your tutor.
4. Compose an e-mail message and enter a title in the Subject box.
5. Enter your own e-mail address in the **Cc:** box.
6. **Send** the message. (If you are working offline you will need to connect to your ISP.)
7. Close your e-mail program.

→ Practise your skills 3

1. Open your e-mail program.
2. Start a new message.
3. Enter the e-mail addresses of someone you know **and** your tutor in the address box.
4. Compose an e-mail message and enter a title in the Subject box.
5. Enter your own e-mail address in the **Bcc:** box.
6. **Send** the message. (If you are working offline you will need to connect to your ISP.)
7. Close your e-mail program

Netiquette

There are very few rules about what you can or cannot do on the Net, but there is general agreement about what is considered good and bad manners. A code of conduct has grown through the increased use of the Net which is often referred to as Netiquette.

Rule 1 Keep it brief. It is common sense to make sure that your e-mails are brief, clear and concise. It takes less time online to send and less time online to download. If you are paying your own phone bill, that could be quite a consideration, especially if you send and receive quite a few e-mails on a regular basis.

Rule 2 Watch what you say and how you say it! It isn't always easy with words on a page, especially written quickly and briefly, to communicate exactly what you want to say. On the phone, you can often tell what people **are not** saying by their tone of voice, but it's difficult to put that into a text message.

There are two ways of communicating feelings on the Net. One is by putting words in brackets to show a little about your mood, e.g. <grin>, <sob>, the other way is to use what's called **emoticons** or **smileys**. These are made up of keyboard characters, which if you look at them sideways appear to be little faces with different expressions. Some examples of emoticons are:

:-D	Laughing	**:-(**	Sad
:-)	Happy	**:-/**	Confused
:-O	Shocked	**;-)**	Wink
:'-)	Crying	**:-l**	Not amused
:-ll	Angry	**>:-)**	Evil grin

There are, of course, many others used by people who send e-mail regularly.

Rule 3 Only use acronyms (where initial letters are used to make up another word – although strictly speaking these aren't acronyms but are commonly referred to as such) that others will understand. The use of acronyms in e-mail messages was popular because it cut down the time spent online composing your message, and of course time costs money. The use of these acronyms has taken off with the increase in text messaging in recent years.

Some common acronyms are:

AFAIK	As far as I know
BCNU	Be seeing you
BTW	By the way
FYI	For your information
FAQ	Frequently asked questions
GAL	Get a life
L8R	See you later
ROFL	Rolls on the floor laughing
TNX	Thanks

Again, there are many more and new ones are joining the list all the time.

Rule 4 Don't shout! ENTERING YOUR TEXT IN CAPITAL LETTERS DOESN'T LOOK VERY FRIENDLY, AND IS TAKEN AS SHOUTING.

Rule 5 Reply promptly. Because e-mail is so quick and easy, people generally expect a reply, even if it's only to say that you've received their e-mail.

Rule 6 Don't forward someone else's e-mail without their permission. After all, you wouldn't like anyone to do that to one of your private messages.

Rule 7 Don't put anything in an e-mail that is strictly private. Anyone can forward your e-mail to a newspaper, your boss at work, or your parents, so use the phone to pass on your message if it's private.

Receiving e-mails

You can change the way Outlook Express looks by using the **Layout** option in the **View** menu. In the screen shot below, the Preview pane is shown with the selected message in view.

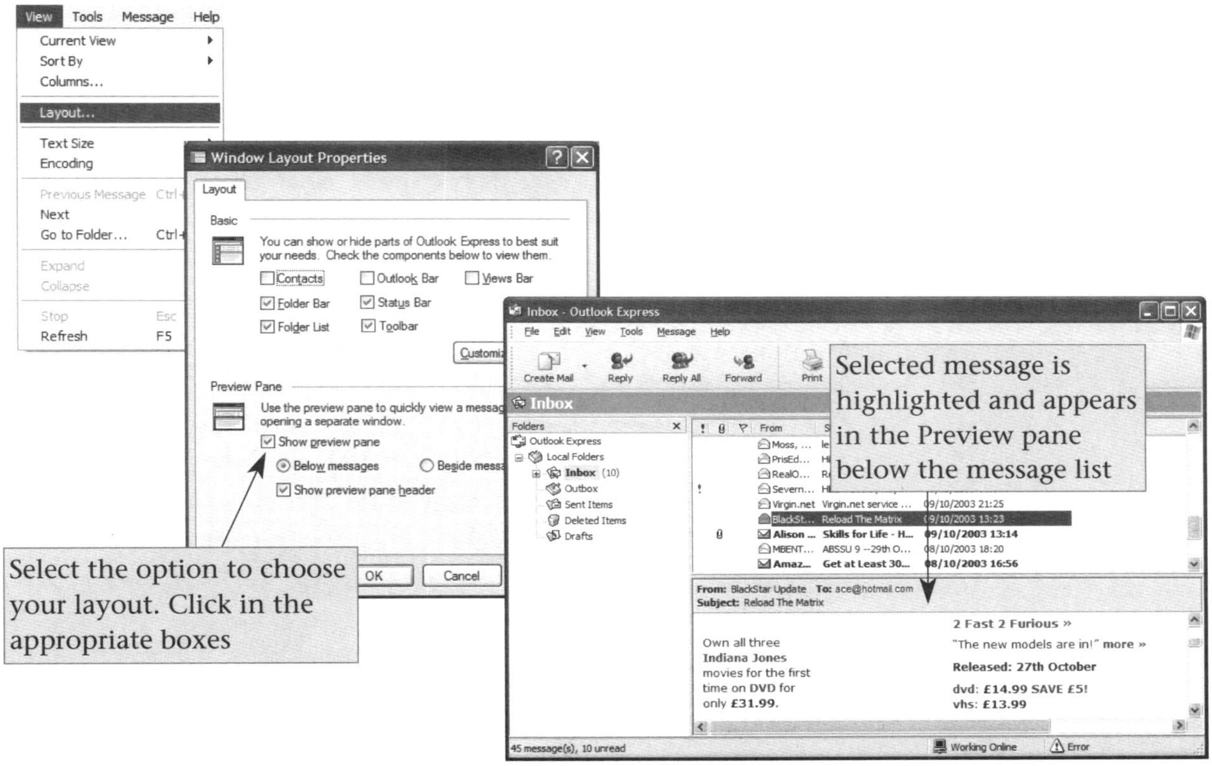

Figure 4.16 Receiving an e-mail

Hint:

If you make changes to your Window Layout Properties but decide that you didn't want to '**Apply**' the changes, you can always click on the **Cancel** button, which will leave the settings as they were before you began.

Task 4.7 Receiving an e-mail

Method

1. Click on the **Send and Receive All** button.
2. Any incoming messages will be placed in your **Inbox** folder.
3. Click on the **Inbox** folder.
4. Select the new message to read it.

This message header gives all the details about the message: From, To, Subject and Date

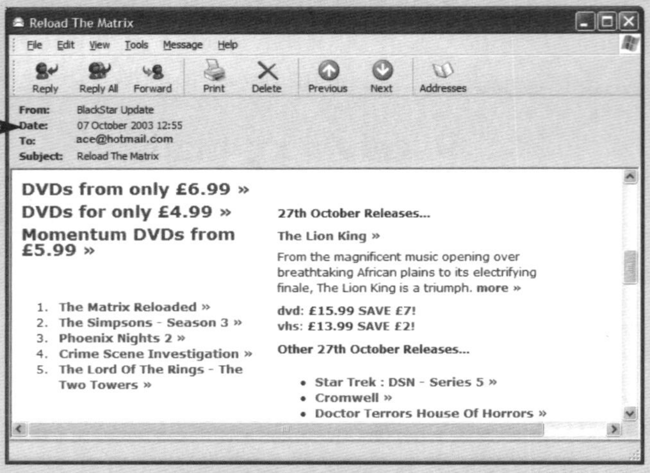

Figure 4.17 Receiving an e-mail message

Hints:

When you receive a new message the **New Message** icon will appear on the status bar. It looks like a sealed envelope.

Your new messages will appear in your Inbox in **bold** type. This changes to a regular typeface when the message has been read.

You can select the message and read it in the Preview pane, or double click on the message and it will open in a separate window as shown in Figure 4.17.

Task 4.8 Deleting e-mails

If you're sending and receiving lots of e-mails, you'll soon find that your Inbox and Sent Items folder gets rather full. When that happens it may be time to delete some of your old messages.

Method

1. Select the e-mail message you want to delete.
2. Click on the **Delete** button on the toolbar, or select the **Delete** option in the **Edit** menu, or use the hotkey combination **Ctrl + D**.
3. The e-mail will be placed in your **Deleted Items** folder. You can open the folder to check it is there.

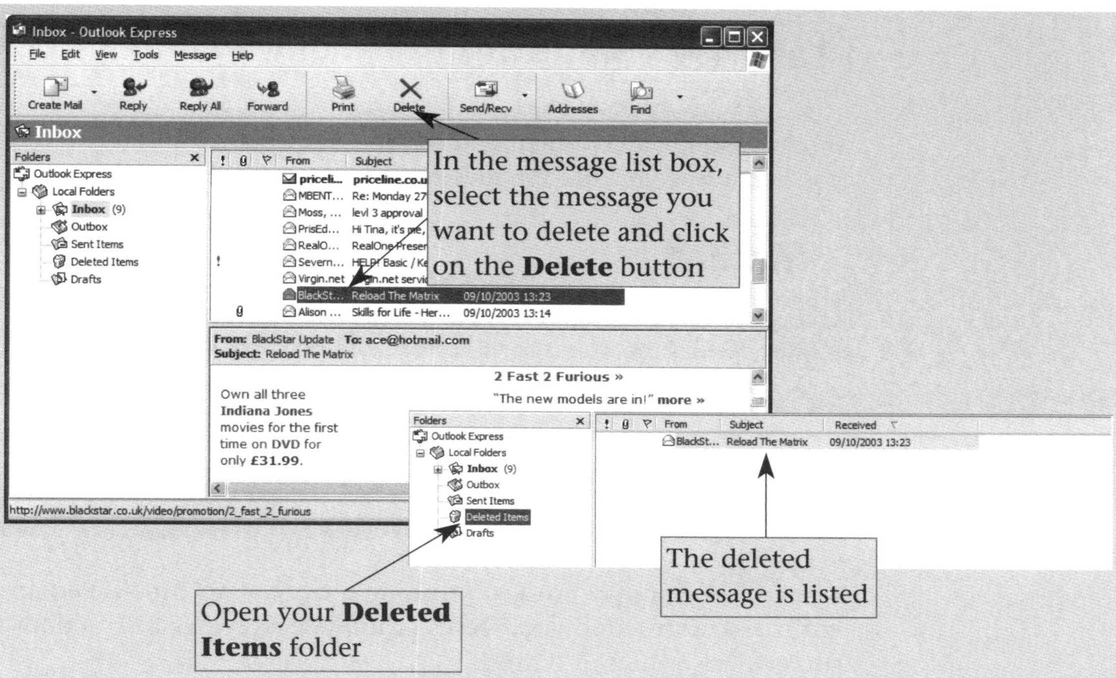

Figure 4.18 Deleting an e-mail message

You may decide that you don't want to keep any of your deleted messages in your Deleted Items folder. Before you close Outlook Express you can do either of the following:

1 Select **Options** from the **Tools** menu.
2 Select the **Maintenance** tab.
3 Check the **Empty messages from the 'Deleted Items' folder on exit** box.

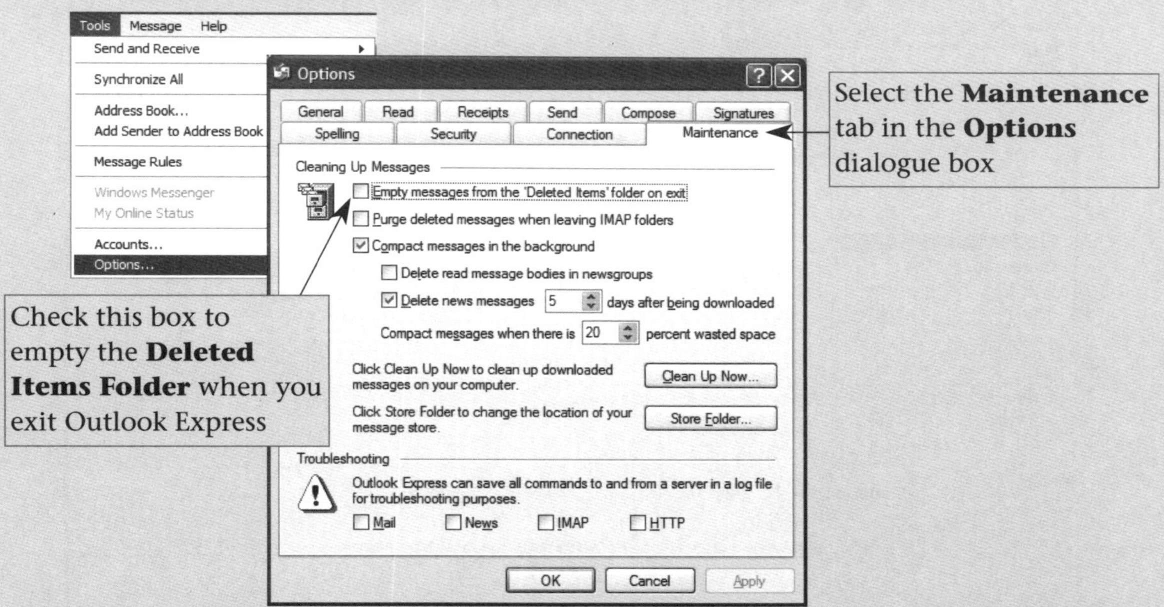

Figure 4.19 One method of removing deleted e-mail messages

or

1 Select the **Empty 'Deleted Items' Folder** from the **Edit** menu on the toolbar.

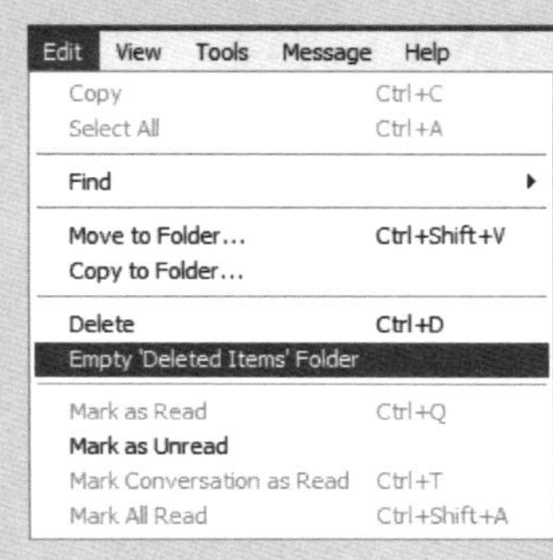

Figure 4.20 Another method of removing deleted e-mail messages

Task 4.9 Restoring a deleted e-mail message

If you've deleted an e-mail and haven't emptied your Deleted Items folder, you can always restore the message.

Method

1. Open the Deleted Items folder.
2. Select the message to restore and hold down the mouse button.
3. Drag the message back to the Inbox or other folder.

Task 4.10 Printing e-mails

Sometimes you may want to print out a copy of an e-mail. Perhaps it contains information you need to complete a task, or instructions to go somewhere or do something.

Method

1. Select the e-mail message you want to print.
2. Click on the **Print** button on the toolbar, or select **Print** from the **File** menu.
3. Check your printer settings.
4. Click on **Print**.

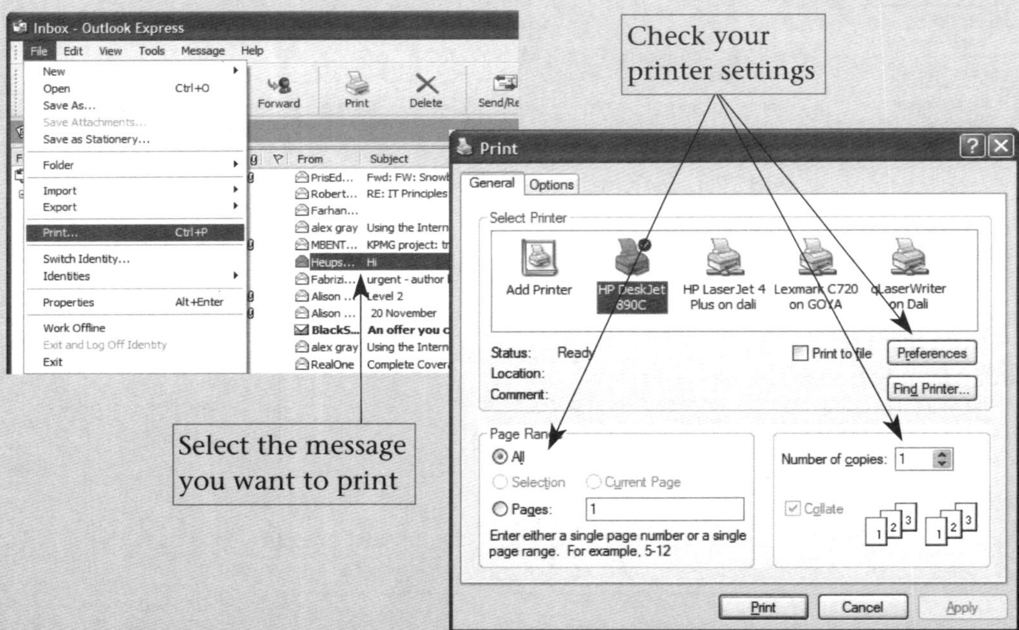

Figure 4.21 Printing an e-mail message

When you print out your e-mail, you will notice that it contains more information than you see in the message pane when you open it. You will find information such as the e-mail address or name of the sender, the e-mail address of you, the recipient, the date and time the e-mail was sent, and the subject of the e-mail.

There is usually a header and a footer on the printout which shows the date the e-mail was printed out and the number of pages in the messages.

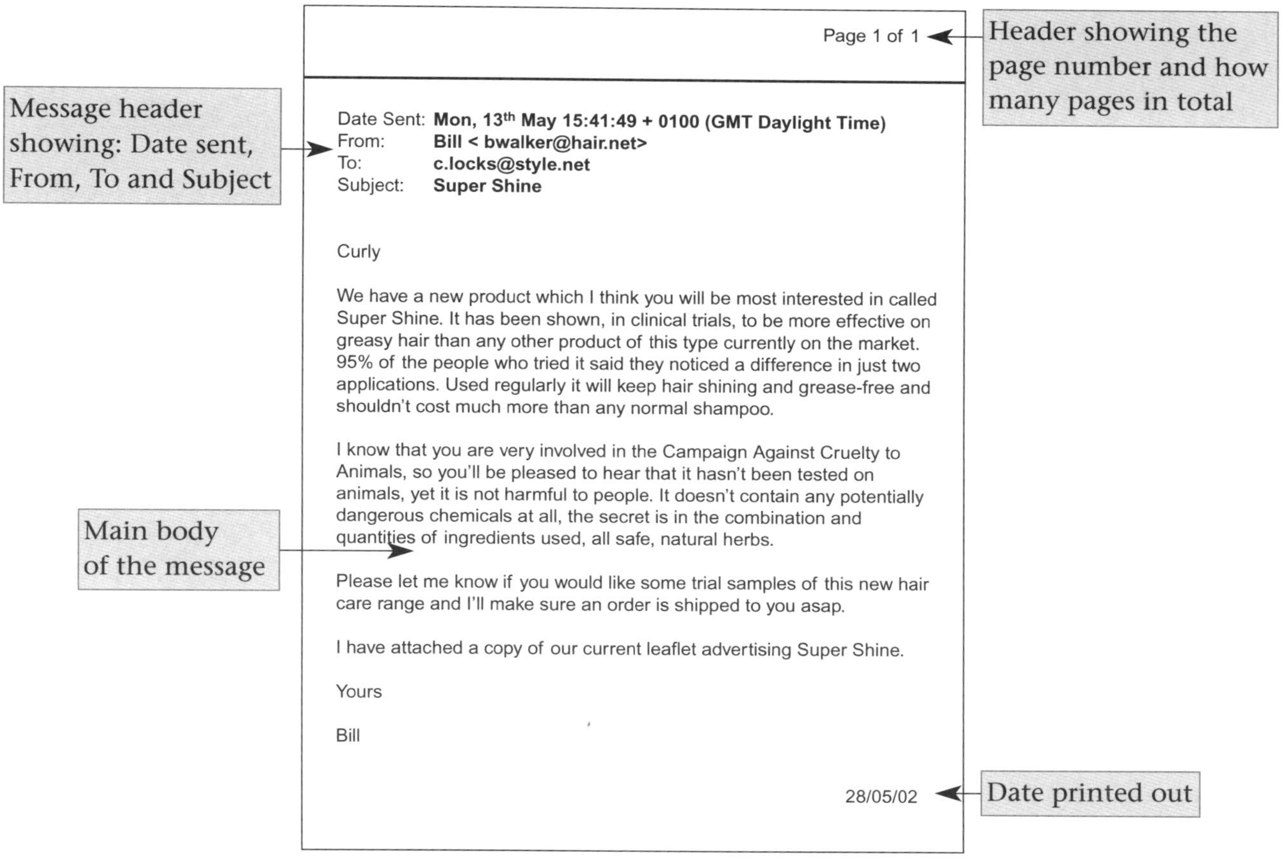
Page 1 of 1

Date Sent: Mon, 13th May 15:41:49 + 0100 (GMT Daylight Time)
From: Bill < bwalker@hair.net>
To: c.locks@style.net
Subject: Super Shine

Curly

We have a new product which I think you will be most interested in called Super Shine. It has been shown, in clinical trials, to be more effective on greasy hair than any other product of this type currently on the market. 95% of the people who tried it said they noticed a difference in just two applications. Used regularly it will keep hair shining and grease-free and shouldn't cost much more than any normal shampoo.

I know that you are very involved in the Campaign Against Cruelty to Animals, so you'll be pleased to hear that it hasn't been tested on animals, yet it is not harmful to people. It doesn't contain any potentially dangerous chemicals at all, the secret is in the combination and quantities of ingredients used, all safe, natural herbs.

Please let me know if you would like some trial samples of this new hair care range and I'll make sure an order is shipped to you asap.

I have attached a copy of our current leaflet advertising Super Shine.

Yours

Bill

28/05/02

Figure 4.22 A printout of an e-mail message

→ Practise your skills 4

1 Open your e-mail program.
2 Check to see if you have any new mail.
3 Read your new mail.
4 Print out a copy.
5 Close your e-mail program.

→ Practise your skills 5

1 Open your e-mail program.
2 Select the message you have received.
3 Print out a copy.
4 Delete the original message 'Sending e-mail'.

Task 4.11 Forwarding an e-mail

One of the advantages of e-mails is that you can forward a message to someone else without having to type it out again. This can be very useful if you have received a message with some information that you need to share with someone else.

Method

1. With the chosen message selected, click on the **Forward** button on the toolbar.
2. In the message window which opens, enter the e-mail address of the person to whom you want to forward the message.
3. If you want to add some text to the message, click in the message box and enter your text.
4. Send the message in the usual way.

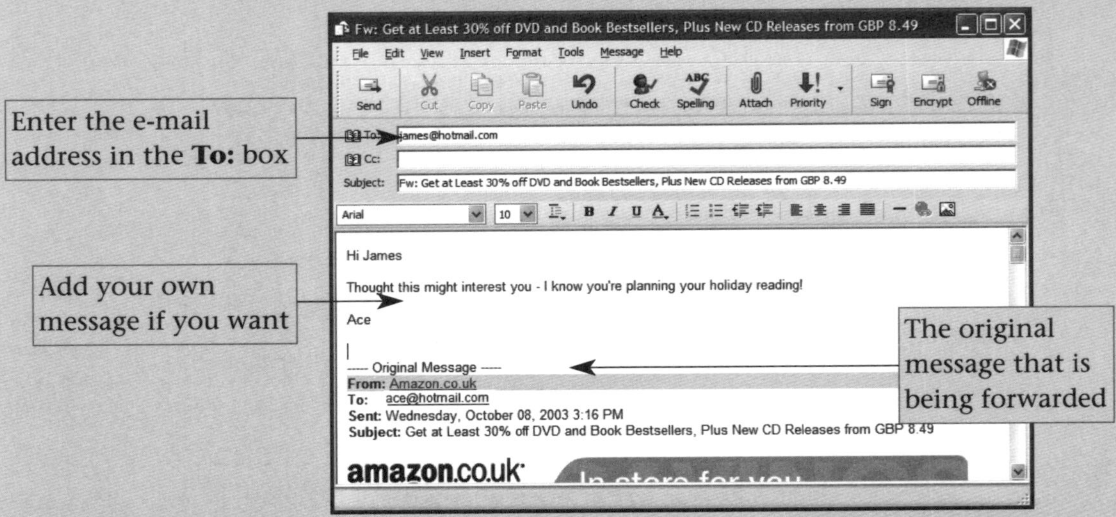

Figure 4.23 Forwarding an e-mail message to someone else

Task 4.12 Replying to e-mails

Another advantage of e-mail is that you can reply to a message very easily. Using the **Reply** function, you can send back a copy of the message without having to type it again, or entering the recipient's address in the Address box. You can even use the same Subject heading, unless you want to change it. You can add your own message to the text and your recipient will have a copy of the original message to refer to.

Method

1. With the chosen message selected, click on the **Reply** button on the toolbar.
2. Click in the message box and enter your text.
3. Send your message in the usual way.

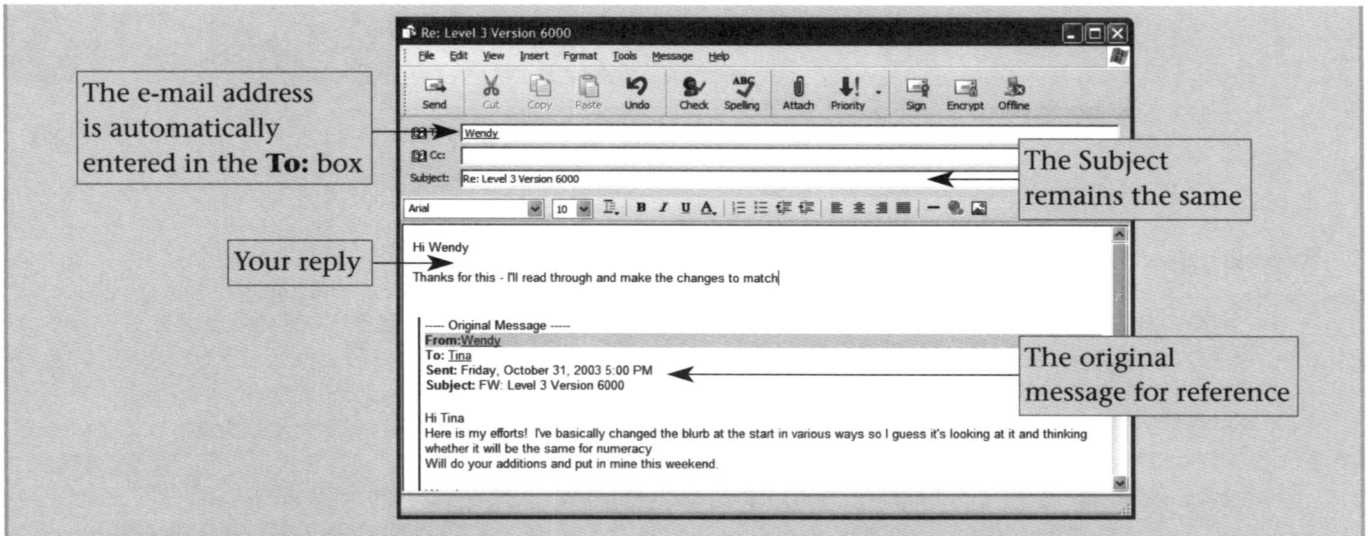

Figure 4.24 Replying to an e-mail message

→ Practise your skills 6

1. Open your e-mail program.
2. Check for new messages.
3. Select one of your messages, forward it to your tutor and send yourself a copy.
4. Select another message, reply to the sender and send a blind carbon copy to yourself.
5. Send your e-mails.
6. Close your e-mail program.

→ Practise your skills 7

1. Open your e-mail program.
2. Check for new messages.
3. Read the blind carbon copy of your message from the previous exercise and print out a copy.
4. Delete the message.
5. Close your e-mail program.

Information

On a network, you will probably find that there is an organisation address list if you click on the **Addresses** button 

. You can use this list to select a name to be entered in the **To:** box of a **New Message** to save you having to type it in yourself!

You can also store your most used addresses in the **Address Book**.

Task 4.13 Saving e-mails

Having received your e-mails, you might want to save an e-mail as a file so that you can open it in another program.

Method

1. Select the message you want to save.
2. Select the **Save As** option from the **File** menu.
3. Enter a name for the file in the **Save As** dialogue box.
4. Choose where you will save the file.
5. Click on **Save**.

Figure 4.25 Saving an e-mail message

Sending attachments

You can **attach** files and documents to your e-mail, which makes it very useful if you want to get your documents to someone more quickly (and often more cheaply) than snail mail. Attachments can include word processing documents, images, sound or video files, and even computer programs. When you send an attachment, your mail program copies the file from wherever it is located and attaches it to your message. You can send more than one file as an attachment, in fact you could send a word processed document, an image and a video clip with the same e-mail, but be warned, an image file might take quite a while to send, and to receive. You may not be too popular with your friends if you keep sending them large files which mean they have to stay online for quite a while waiting for the files to download!

Task 4.14 Sending e-mail attachments

Method

1. Load your e-mail program.
2. Click on the **Create Mail** button on the toolbar.
3. Enter the e-mail address, the subject and your message.
4. Click on the **Attach File** button 

on the toolbar.
5. The **Insert Attachment** window appears.
6. Select the drive where the file you wish to send has been saved.
7. Click on the file, so that it appears in the **File name** box.
8. Click on **Attach**.
9. Your file will be shown in the **Attach:** box of your message.
10. **Send** the e-mail.

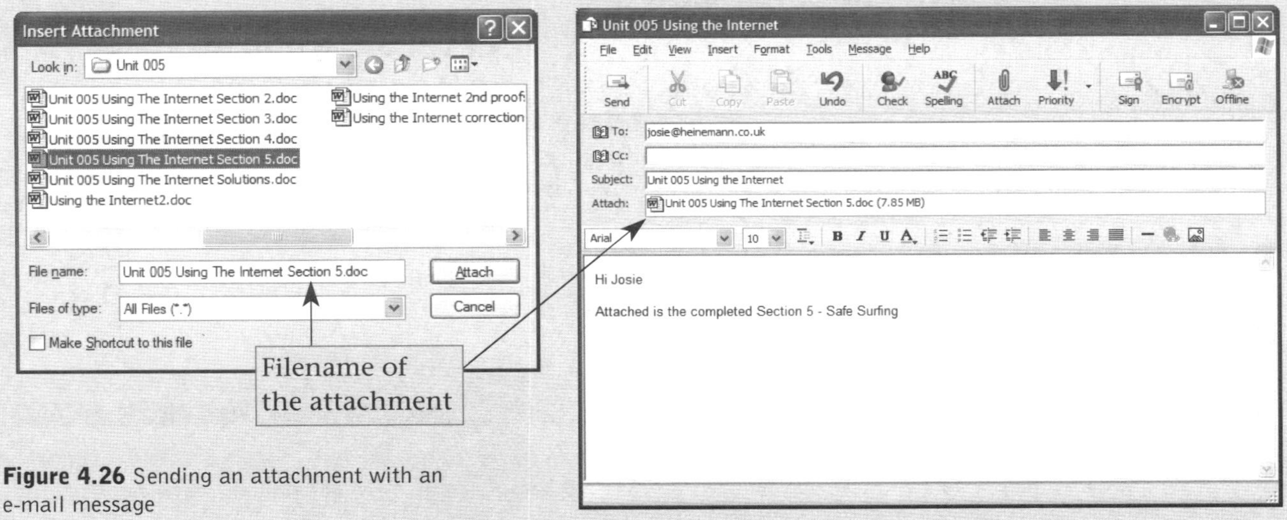

Figure 4.26 Sending an attachment with an e-mail message

Hint:

You can also copy and paste information from documents into a message, in just the same way that you could do in any other program.

Receiving attachments

E-mails can also be sent to you with an attachment. You will need to take great care opening any such files you receive as they can carry viruses. It is important to scan any e-mail attachment with a virus checker before you open it. Just as with sending attachments, you could receive documents, images, video or music clips, and programs attached to e-mails.

When you receive an attachment, the message is displayed in the message list with a paper clip icon next to it. When you receive an attachment you have two choices: to save it as a file or to open it.

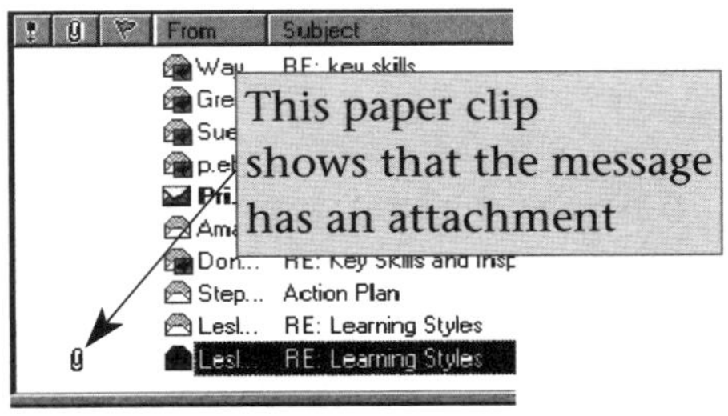

Figure 4.27 Receiving an e-mail with an attachment

Hint:

You may find that you want to delete an attachment because you've made a mistake and attached the wrong file prior to sending an e-mail. Simply select the file icon in the message header and press **Delete** on the keyboard. Now you can try again, and attach the file you really wanted to send!

Task 4.15 Viewing your attachment

Method 1

1 In the Preview pane, your attachment will be shown as a paper clip in the top right-hand corner of the pane.
2 Click on the paper clip and you will see the filename and an option to save the attachment.
3 Click on the filename and the **Open Attachment Warning** dialogue box appears. Select the **Open it** option and it will open – provided you have a program on your computer which will open files of the type sent!
4 View the attachment and then close your program in the usual way.

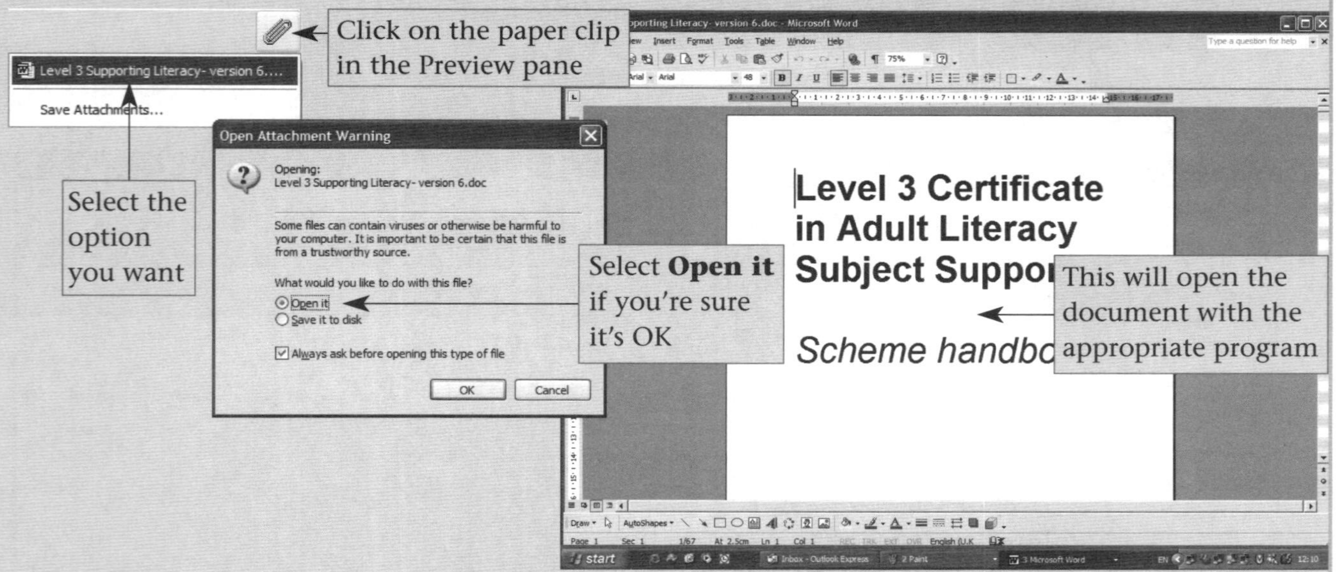

Figure 4.28 Viewing an attachment

Method 2

1 Double click on the message in the message list.
2 Double click on the file attachment in the message header.
3 Select the **Open it** option from the **Open Attachment Warning** dialogue box. This will open the file in the appropriate program.
4 View the attachment and then close your program in the usual way.

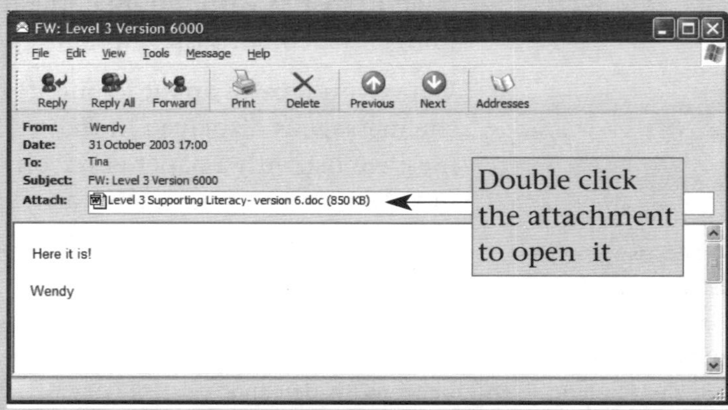

Figure 4.29 Another method of viewing an attachment

Remember:

A plain text e-mail doesn't carry a virus – it's only the attachments which do that. That is why it is so important to virus check any attachments you receive *before* you open them.

Task 4.16 Saving attachments

You may want to save your attachments to your hard disk and look at them later.

Method 1

1 In the Preview pane, your attachment will be shown as a paper clip in the top right-hand corner of the pane.
2 Click on the paper clip and you will see the filename and an option to save the attachment.
3 Click on the **Save Attachments** option.
4 Browse your hard drive to find where you want to save your attachment, and click **Save**.

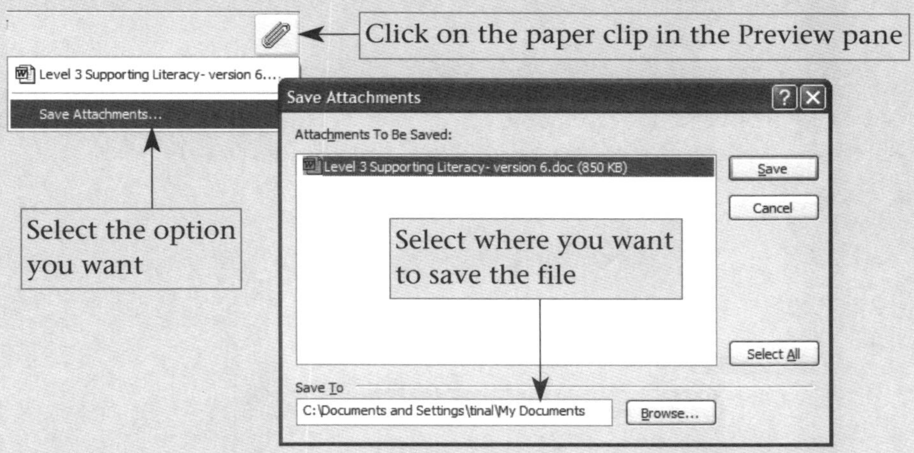

Figure 4.30 Saving an attachment

Method 2

1 Double click on the message in the message list.
2 Select **Save Attachments** from the **File** menu.
3 Browse your hard drive to find where you want to save your attachment, and click **Save**.

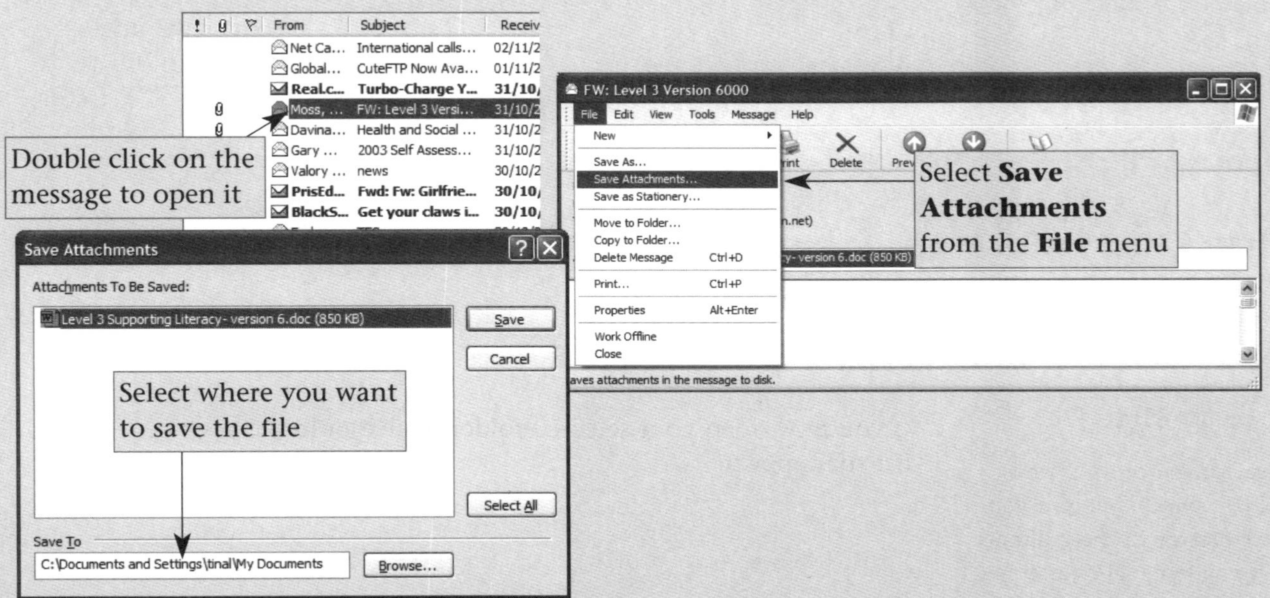

Figure 4.31 Another method of saving an attachment

Managing your folders

Just as you sometimes need to sort out your paper correspondence, so you might need to tidy up and organise your e-mail folders. This can be a helpful way to get your mail sorted into different categories, such as: mail from friends, from work, or from family. You will have already found out that deleting files you no longer want can help to keep your folders tidy (see Task 4.8).

Task 4.17 Creating a new folder

Method

1 Right mouse click on one of the folders in the Folders list (e.g. Inbox).
2 Select **New Folder** from the pop-up menu.
3 Enter the name you wish to give to the new folder in the **Folder name** box.

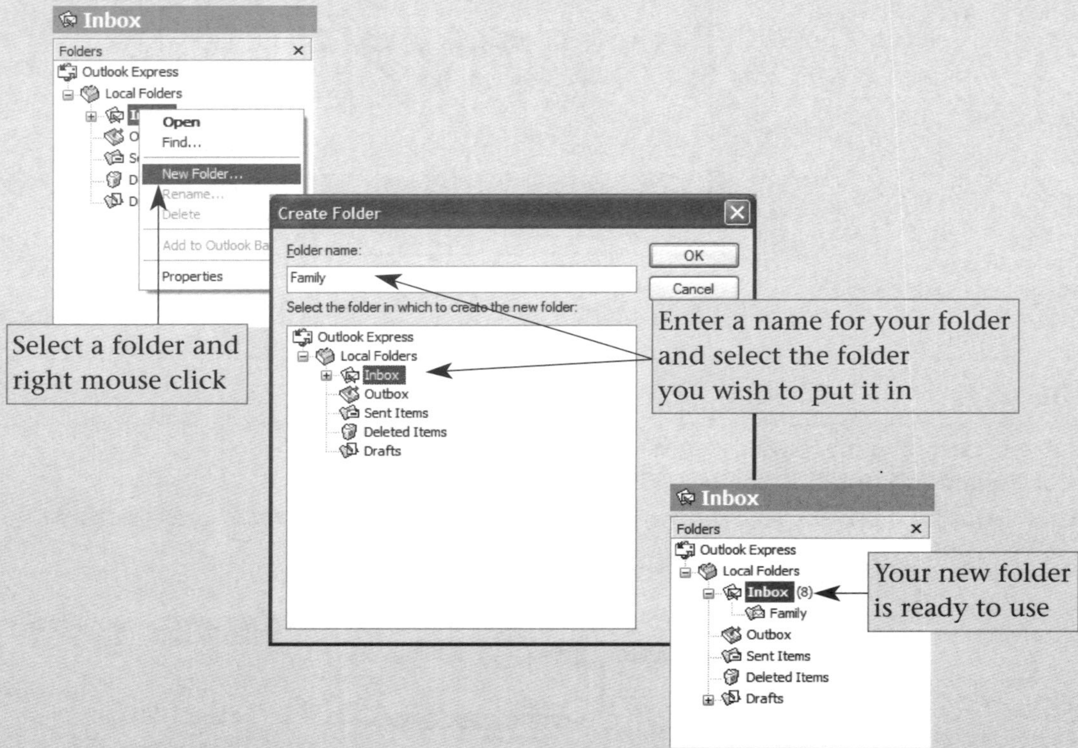

Figure 4.32 Creating a new folder

4 Select the folder you wish to create the new folder in.
5 Click on **OK**.

Hint:

Use names for your new folders which will give you an indicator of the contents – it can make life easier later when you're searching for a particular e-mail.

If you now open your selected folder, you should see your new folder in the list that appears.

Task 4.18 Moving messages into a folder

Having created a new folder, you can now move messages into it.

Method

1. Right mouse click on the message you wish to move.
2. Select **Move to Folder** from the pop-up menu.
3. Select the folder you want to move the message to.
4. Click on **OK**.

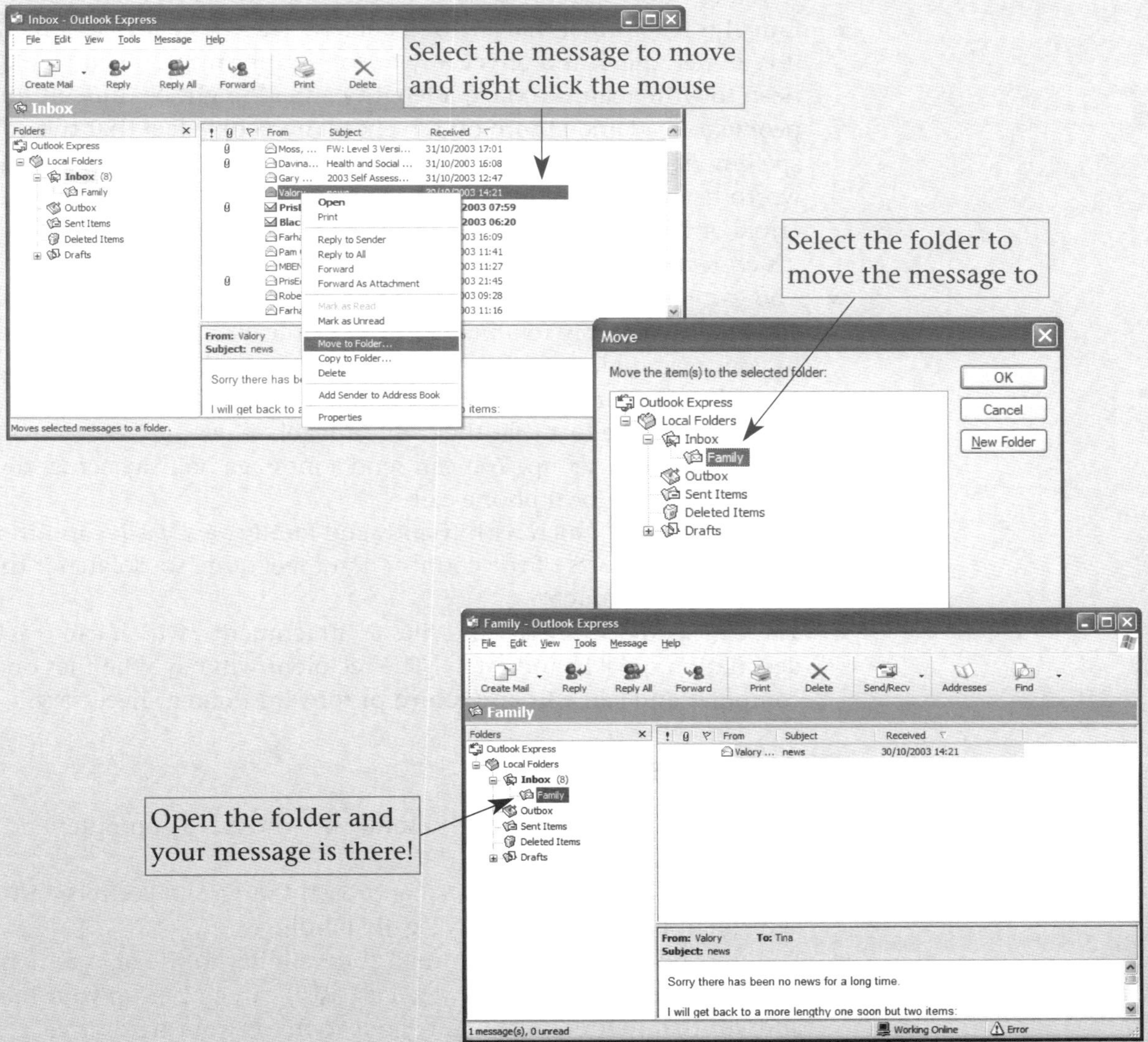

Figure 4.33 Moving an e-mail message to a folder

Hint:

You can also copy a message to another folder using this method, but choosing the **Copy to Folder** option.

If you open the folder, your message should now be shown in the message list.

Hint:

If you have both the message list and the folder list in view, you can also click on the message, hold down the mouse button and drag the message to the appropriate folder.

Pros and cons of using e-mail

E-mail is a quick, cheap way of keeping in touch with other people, but like any system, it has its good points and bad points.

Advantages

- It is almost instantaneous. Mail is sent immediately you click the Send button without having to walk to the Post Box or remember to buy a stamp. Your message should get to the recipient very shortly after it is sent and they can reply as soon as they have checked their e-mail box.
- E-mail is less formal than writing a letter. The whole idea of e-mail is that it is a brief, quick and direct way of communicating, so you wouldn't need to write reams. In fact, a lengthy e-mail might be difficult for some people to read and absorb on screen. Many people feel that the odd spelling or punctuation error doesn't matter in an e-mail, although it's worth trying to proof read your e-mails quickly to see if you can spot errors or typos (typing errors). It makes it easier for the receiver to read if it's correct.
- You can reply to an e-mail without having to type in the recipient's address. If you reply to an e-mail, you can leave a copy of their message in your own e-mail so they don't have to search for the original one.
- It can be cheaper than sending a message by snail mail, especially taking into account the fact that they will probably have the hardware and software already set up. You can send a message halfway across the world for the cost of a local phone call.
- You can keep in touch with friends and family very easily, and those who live in remote parts of the country don't feel quite so isolated if they are able to keep in touch.
- You can send documents and files as attachments, which can reach their destination quickly and safely. The recipient will have the files on their computer and can edit and return or forward them as necessary.

Disadvantages

- You can only send an e-mail to someone who has a computer and an ISP account.
- E-mails may have a more casual approach than formal letters, but an agreement by e-mail is just as legally binding.
- You may find that junk mail (mail shots similar to the ones which come through your letter box on a regular basis!) can clutter up your Inbox, and, for that matter, take up precious room on your hard drive.
- There is always the risk of catching a virus from an attachment. People distribute viruses to make mischief and, if they have access to a mailing list of e-mail addresses, may just send you an e-mail complete with a nasty surprise if you don't make a habit of virus checking all the attachments you receive.
- To communicate by e-mail is quick and easy, but it does depend on the recipient checking their Inbox regularly. If your e-mails remain on an ISP's server, then it's not really much help to you if you need a reply.

Can you think of any other advantages or disadvantages to add to this list?

→ Practise your skills 8

1. Open your word processing program and enter the following text:

   'You should always use a virus checker when you receive an attachment to check that it is safe to open. If you don't you might find that you have caught a virus which could corrupt your files on your hard drive or, even worse, trash your hard disk completely. It's better to be safe than sorry.'
2. Save your file with the name **Virus Reminder**.
3. Open your e-mail program and enter your own e-mail address in the To: box.
4. Enter a suitable word or phrase in the Subject box.
5. Attach your file **Virus Reminder**.
6. Enter a suitable message in the message section.
7. Send the e-mail in the usual way.
8. Check to see if you've got new mail (hopefully your own file should be placed in your Inbox).
9. Save the attachment in a different location to the one you used before.
10. Open the attachment and print out a copy.
11. Close your e-mail program and disconnect.

Did you remember to virus check the attachment before you opened or saved it? Full marks if you did!

→ Practise your skills 9

1. Open your e-mail program.
2. Enter the e-mail address of someone you know or your tutor.
3. Enter an appropriate title in the Subject box.
4. Attach your file **Virus Reminder**
5. Enter a message in the message section, and include the reason why you are sending the message and ask for an acknowledgement. Ask if they will send you an attachment in return.
6. Set the message as High Priority.
7. Send the e-mail in the usual way.
8. Close your e-mail program and disconnect.

→ Practise your skills 10

1. Open your e-mail program.
2. Check to see if you have any new mail.
3. If you receive a reply to your e-mail with an attachment, save the attachment to your hard drive.
4. Open the attachment and print out a copy.
5. Close your e-mail program and disconnect.
6. Open the program which is associated with the attachment you have received and load your saved file.
7. Print out a copy.
8. Close the program.

→ Practise your skills 11

1 Open your e-mail program.
2 Create a new folder called 'Learning' in your Inbox.
3 Move the messages you have received whilst completing the exercises in this section to the new folder.
4 Close your e-mail program.

→ Check your knowledge

1 Identify the functions of the buttons on the Outlook Express toolbar shown below.

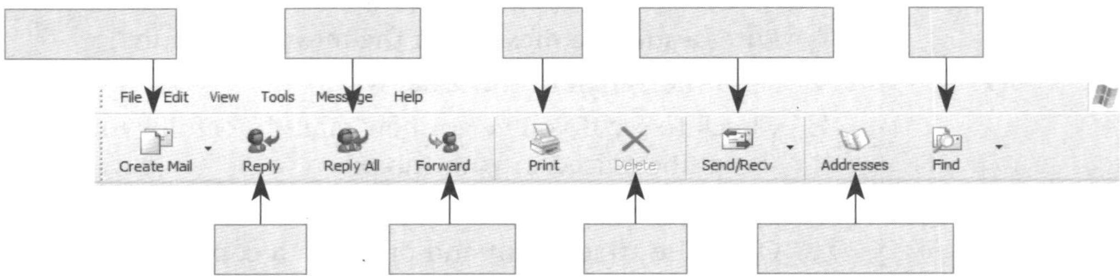

Figure 4.34 Functions of a toolbar

2 What are the advantages of web-based e-mail?
3 What equipment do you need to send e-mails?
4 Identify the components of this e-mail address:

ace@college.ac.uk

5 What would you expect to find in:
- **a** your Inbox
- **b** your Sent Items folder
- **c** your Deleted Items folder.

6 If you wanted to send a copy of your message to someone without the recipient knowing, what function would you use?
7 Why should you never enter your text message in capital letters?
8 How can you tell which messages you have read from those you haven't read?
9 What might you send as an attachment?
10 Why might you want to manage your folders in Outlook Express?

Consolidation

1. Load your browser and connect to your ISP.
2. Use a search engine, a directory and a meta search site to locate information about your star sign and that of a friend or relative.
3. Choose the information you think is best and save the web pages to an appropriate location. Save any images separately.
4. Create a folder with the name **Astrology** in your Favorites folder.
5. Save the web site addresses to the **Astrology** folder.
6. Use one of the search methods to locate a horoscope for yourself and your friend for today.
7. Print out a copy of each horoscope reading.
8. Disconnect from the Net, but don't close your browser.
9. Open your e-mail program.
10. Start a new e-mail message to your friend using appropriate stationery. Enter the heading **Your Stars Today** in the Subject box and send a carbon copy to yourself.
11. Enter a suitable message in the message box saying that you are attaching the web pages with the information about your friend's star sign. Attach the appropriate files from the saved location.
12. From your browser's History folder, copy the URL of the horoscope for your friend and paste it into your e-mail message with a suitable comment.
13. Connect to your ISP.
14. Send the message, disconnect from your ISP and close your e-mail program.
15. Locate the saved file with your own star sign information and open it. Print out a copy.
16. Close your browser.

Section 5 Safe surfing

You will learn to

- Set security features and identify the reasons for using them:
  - ☐ virus protection
  - ☐ locks
  - ☐ alerts
  - ☐ digital signatures
  - ☐ passwords
- Identify the types of information that may be protected by copyright:
  - ☐ music
  - ☐ shareware
  - ☐ software
  - ☐ graphics

Security

The Internet has a wealth of information and services to offer the intrepid surfer, and the value of being able to communicate via e-mail quickly and easily cannot be in doubt, but there are negative sides to the Internet. Viruses, security breaches and bugs are a threat to people's private information, files and even their computer. Security concerns everyone who uses a computer, whether at home or at work. There are some simple measures you can take to protect against intrusions into your private computing life.

Viruses

A virus can be a threat to your files and your computer itself. These are specially devised programs that can cause havoc with your data. They can be placed in an e-mail attachment or on a downloaded file from the Internet. However they travel, it is vital to have your virus checker installed, up-dated regularly and active. Most commercial software has features that you can set to monitor all files which pass through your Internet connection, as well as checking your e-mails. If any viruses are detected, you will get a warning dialogue box which will alert you to a possible virus infection. Some commercial software will allow you to 'quarantine' the file, making sure it doesn't infect your computer, and then send it to the program developers so they can investigate it and decide if it is a new virus. This helps them to keep their virus definitions up to date.

These following screen shots from a commercially available anti-virus utility show some of the options available. These options can be set by checking or unchecking the appropriate boxes.

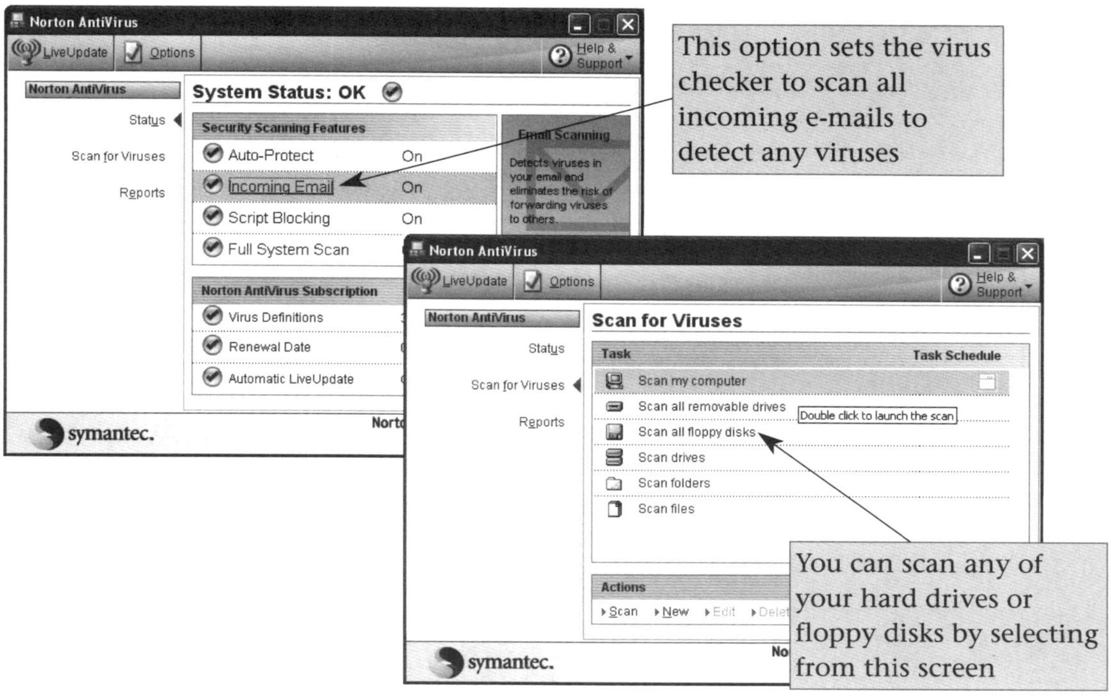

Figure 5.1 An anti-virus utility

Hint:

Most commercial anti-virus programs will allow you to connect to their web site to update your virus checks regularly. The program will often have a reminder to do this set to alert you to the need to update the virus checker at pre-set periods. Ignore it at your peril!

Task 5.1 Setting your safety level

Your browser and e-mail programs have security features which will also help in the fight against viruses. In the Internet Options dialogue box you can specify how Internet Explorer should handle the downloading of files, depending on where they have come from.

Method

1. Select **Internet Options** from the **Tools** menu.
2. Select the **Security** tab.

You will see that four security zones are shown:

Figure 5.2 Security zones

You can assign different levels of security to each zone.

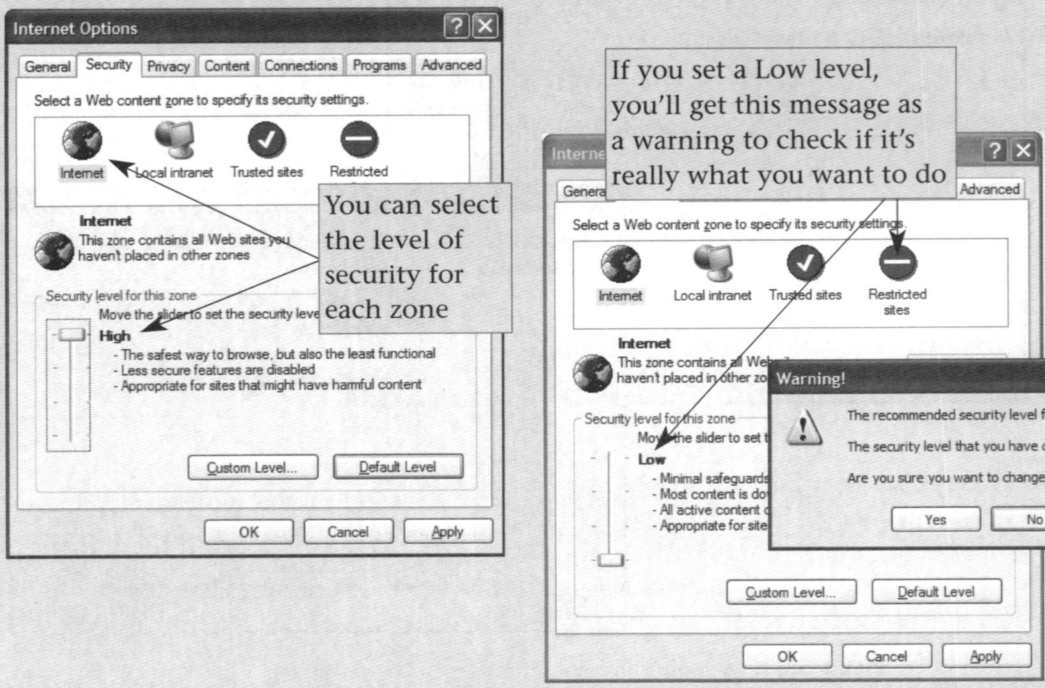

Figure 5.3 Levels of security

The higher the level of security, the less likely you are to be able to download files containing a virus. You can add sites to all of the zones except the Internet one, which contains all the sites not listed in any other category.

3 Select the levels of security which you feel are appropriate for your needs.

Information

If you set the **Medium** option you will be asked for permission before possible unsafe files are downloaded.

Outlook Express shares the settings with Internet Explorer and has a similar function, as shown in the screen shot below:

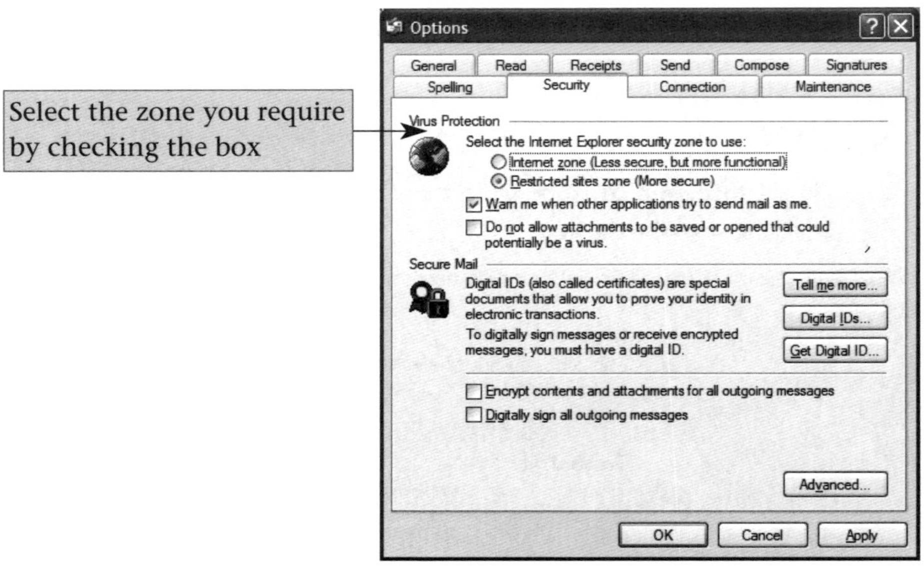

Figure 5.4 Selecting the security zone

Cookies

In computer terms these can be both a benefit and a nuisance. Some web sites you may visit store information as a small text file on your computer. These are called **cookies**. Internet sites use them to store personal information about such things as your preferences when visiting their site. This might be the particular pages you visited or your name if you entered it into any boxes whilst at the site. When you next log on to the site your computer sends the cookie to the site and you may find a message appearing which says 'Hello, Josie. Welcome back.' Cookies can't be used to read data from your hard drive, to pass on your personal details or to make sure the software on your machine has been registered. They are not really harmful, although you may not want them cluttering up your hard drive.

One way of making sure that all cookies don't settle themselves on your hard drive is to set the levels of privacy to suit you. For example, you might want to allow some web sites to create cookies or to prompt you to ask for permission.

Information

You can change your computer settings to disable cookies being stored on your computer by using the **Internet Options**. By selecting the **Privacy** tab and moving the **Settings** slider, you can block all cookies or allow certain validated cookies to settle on your hard drive. You can also set the cookie handling option for individual web sites using the **Edit** button.

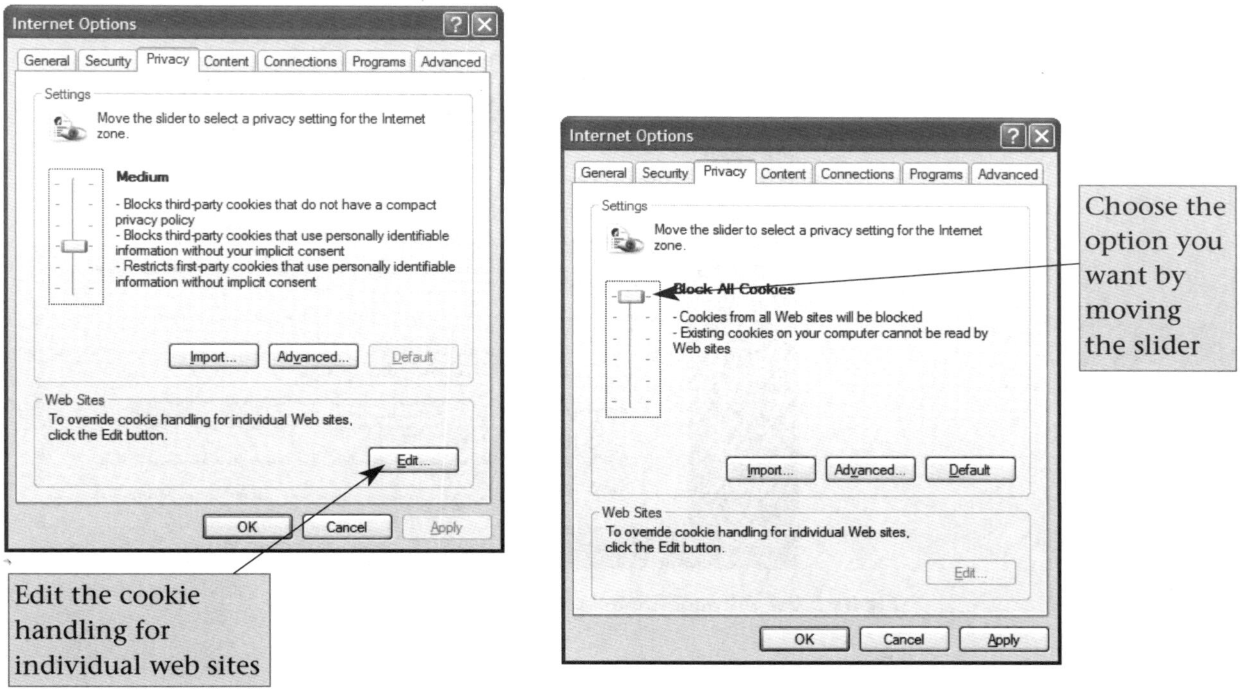

Figure 5.5 Changing cookie settings

Firewalls

When you connect to the Net there is always a chance that you may inadvertently download a file with a virus or allow a hacker to access your computer through your connection. However, if you are using your phone line at home and your virus checking software regularly, you are fairly safe from attack. Hackers are people who enjoy working with computer codes and programming, and some will break into other people's systems to access data or alter files. With the increasing use of cable broadband and ISDN connections, which are permanently connected to the Internet, your computer is much more vulnerable to attack. Firewalls are a possible way of protecting against such intrusion. They provide a system that prevents unauthorised access to a computer over a network, such as the Internet. Firewalls can be either hardware or software. Businesses will tend to use a hardware firewall, whereas a home user will probably use software.

A firewall will check every bit of data that goes in and out of your computer, to ensure that only acceptable data ends up on your machine. Firewalls may also detect viruses, which can save a lot of problems if you forget to update your virus checker.

The screen shot below shows a software firewall program which can be downloaded from the Internet. With this type of program you can set your security levels with various options and completely lock your computer to any Internet activity if a set period of time has passed since any activity was monitored. This can be very useful if you have a permanent connection to the Internet which you may not be accessing all the time.

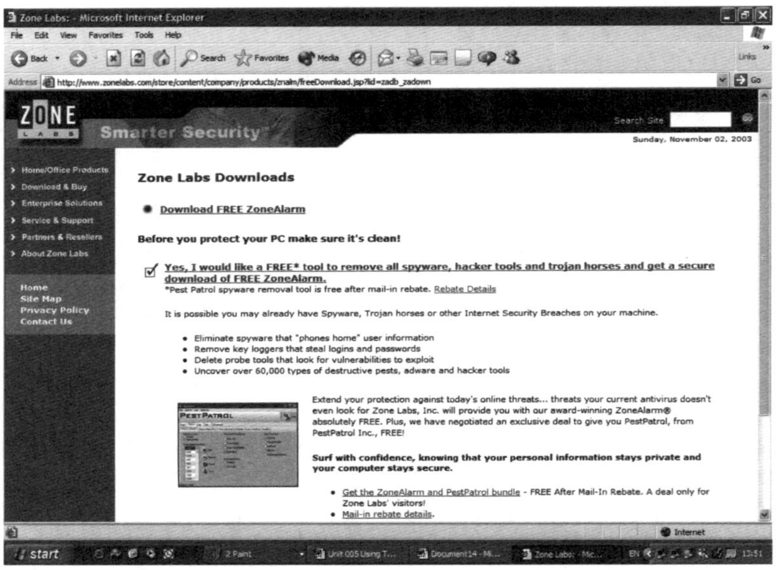

Figure 5.6 A software firewall program

Buying online

Security of personal information is one of the greatest concerns people have about shopping online, or transacting any other business via the Net. Credit card fraud is one of the biggest worries for many people who may otherwise use the Net for commerce. However, taking some reasonable, common sense precautions and using the security measures available should make buying online as safe as handing your credit card to the waiter in a restaurant.

Some rules to help:

- Keep any records of transactions, such as e-mail confirmation of order.
- Provide only the minimum information required. Some of the fields in a personal information form are not compulsory; so only complete those that are.
- Always check that the web site is secure. You can tell if it is by the closed lock icon in Internet Explorer (or the unbroken key icon in Netscape) which appears on your status bar. If you set your Internet Options to warn you if you enter or leave a secure site, you will see alerts similar to those shown below. (This setting is the default setting so you shouldn't need to change it.) As your data is encrypted (scrambled so that no one else can read it) when you send it to a secure site, your details should be safe.

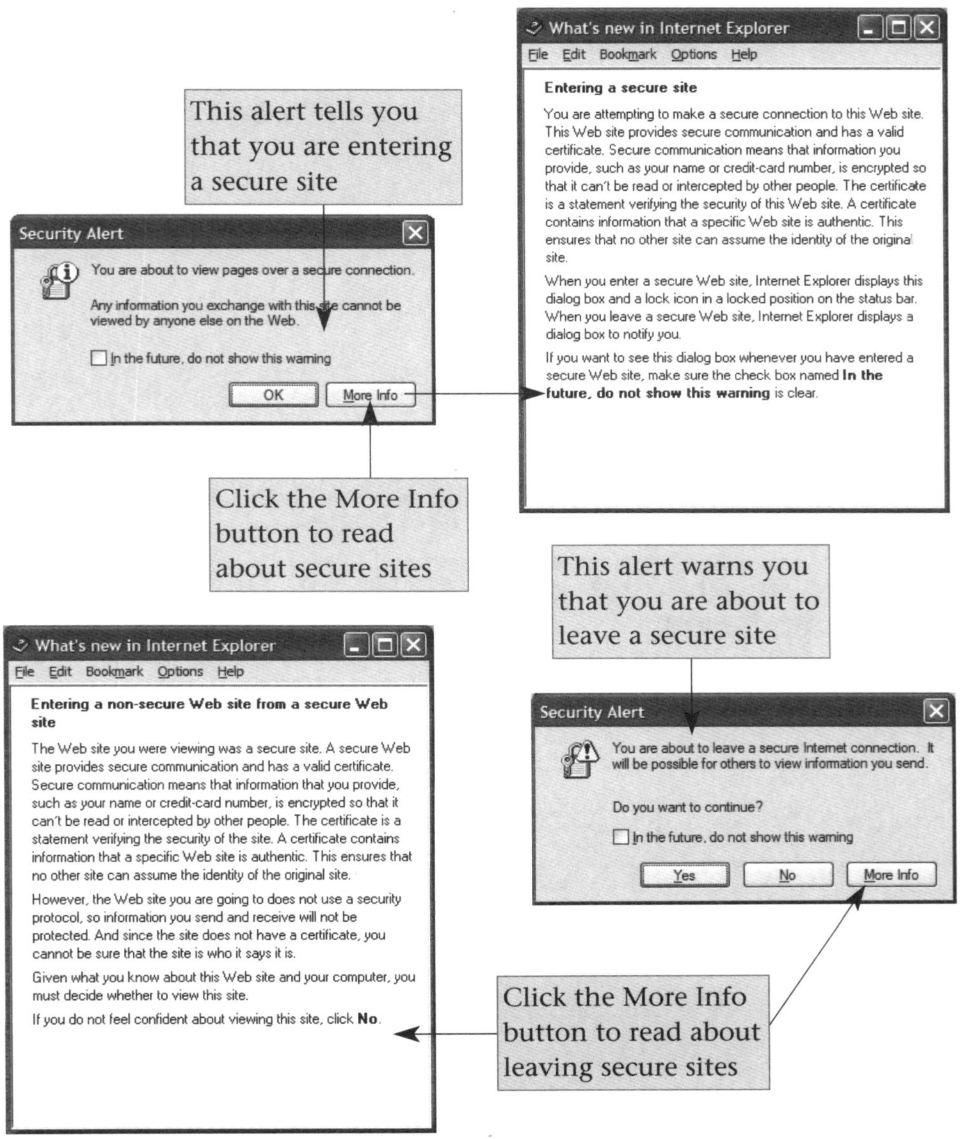

Figure 5.7 Security alerts

Content Advisor

Alongside the excellent information and services available on the Net, there is some very unpleasant material. You can alter your settings in Internet Explorer to control the access to some web sites containing unacceptable material. These settings are available in the **Content Advisor** section of the Internet Options.

Task 5.2 Setting your Content Advisor levels

Method

1. Select **Internet Options** from the **Tools** menu.
2. Click on the **Content** tab.
3. In the **Content Advisor** section, click on **Enable**.
4. Set up the levels you require for each of the headings:
   – Language
   – Nudity
   – Sex
   – Violence
   by dragging the sliders with your mouse.
5. Click on **Apply**.

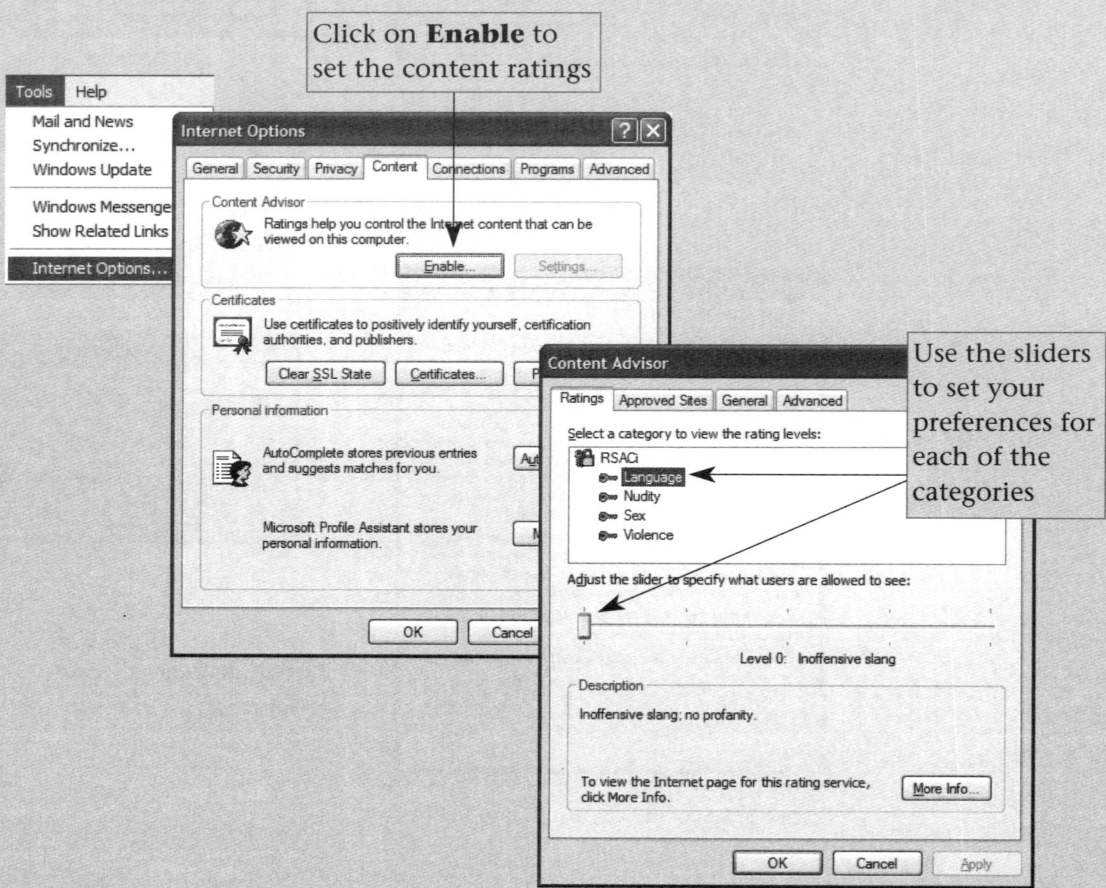

Figure 5.8 Setting Content Advisor levels

Digital signatures

As more people send information by e-mail, it is becoming increasingly important that your e-mails can't be read by anyone other than your recipient. It is vital in the business world to have a system to ensure that no one can pretend to be you and send information under your name which may be false or misleading. This can be done using **digital IDs** or **signatures**.

Using digital IDs in Outlook Express can prove your identity in electronic transactions, as in using your passport when you change foreign currency. You can also use a digital ID to encrypt (code) your e-mails so that only the intended recipient, who knows the code, will be able to read the message.

Digital IDs are issued by independent certification authorities, which will need to verify that you are who you say you are! You do this by entering your personal details on a form on their web site. They will then send you instructions on installing your digital ID. You can then use this to 'sign' your e-mails and ensure that your messages are secure.

Passwords

As you surf the Net, you will no doubt come across sites that require you to sign in with your username or e-mail address and your password.

Figure 5.9 Some sites require you to identify yourself

This will allow you to access parts of the site not otherwise available, for example, or pick up your web-based e-mail. This is your best defence against anyone else accessing your personal account without authority. With this protection comes certain responsibilities and it is important that you choose and safeguard your passwords carefully. A web site can only check that a password entered is one which it can accept; it cannot tell whether the person entering it is you!

Some rules to follow when using passwords:

Rule 1 Don't use passwords that consist of easily obtainable personal information, such as your date of birth, your phone number, your own name or your pet's name.

Rule 2 Think up passwords which have at least six characters which have some letters and numbers mixed together, for example 3fr&7n. A random password like this makes it much harder for someone else to guess.

Rule 3 Use a different password for each service you register with. If you have registered with all the services under one password someone may get hold of that password and be able to access all your accounts.

Rule 4 If you find that you've got a number of passwords and it's getting difficult to remember which one registers with which site, make a note of them, but keep it somewhere secure. Do not leave it lying on the top of your desk, or pinned to the notice board above your head!

Rule 5 Never tell anyone your password.

Rule 6 Change your passwords regularly, especially for sensitive sites such as your online bank.

There are other passwords that can keep your data safe. You will have a password to log on to Windows when you first start up your computer and you can set this password to activate when your screensaver kicks in.

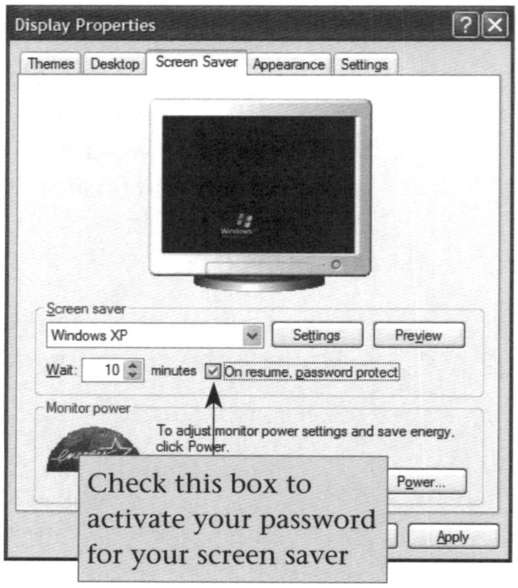

Figure 5.10 Setting passwords

There is the password you use to connect to your ISP. You can check the 'Save password' box, but it would be much safer to be prompted to enter it every time you want to log on.

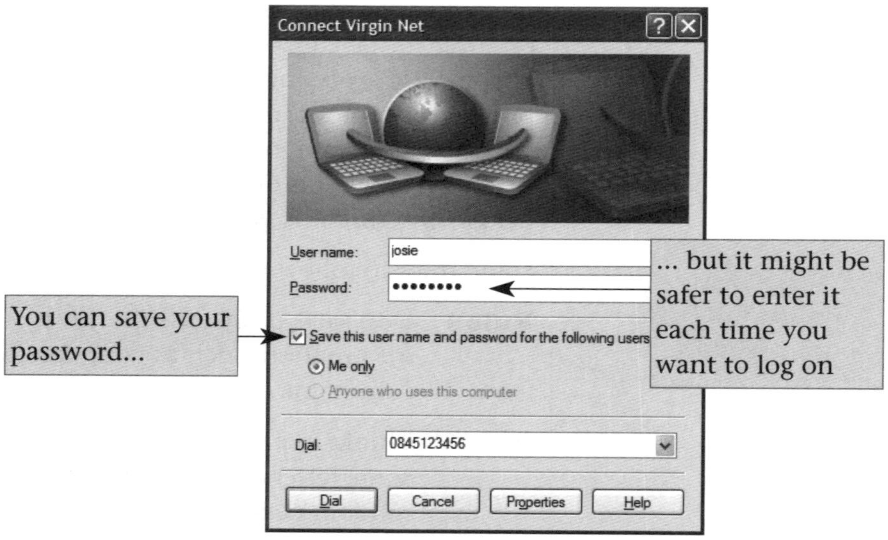

Figure 5.11 Using your password to log on to your ISP

There are programs available which will save and manage your passwords for you, but sometimes old-fashioned pen and pencil is just as easy.

Copyright

Copyright legally protects the work of an author or artist. Information under copyright cannot be used without asking the author for permission.

Software programs have a copyright. It is illegal to copy them without permission and you may have to pay a large fine if you are caught. This is because software is very costly to produce as it takes many hundreds of hours of developers' time to write the programs. When you buy software you buy a licence to use it, not the software itself, which is why it is illegal to copy someone else's software to load on your own machine. An organisation called FAST (Federation Against Software Theft) has been set up by the major software developers to detect and stop illegal copying of software.

There are different licences available and you should always read the small print to check what you can do. Some of the licences available are:

- **Single-user licence** – only for use on one machine at a time.
- **Multi-user licence** – for use on an agreed number of machines, e.g. in a small business.
- **Site licence** – can be used by all users within a site, e.g. in a college or university.

Some software can be used freely, others can only be used under certain conditions.

- **Shareware** This is usually distributed free, and can often be found on the CDs distributed with computer magazines or on web sites. Quite often you can use the software for a specified period of time to try it out, but pay a fee if you decide to keep it. Sometimes this software is distributed with some of the functions disabled or it may have an expiry time set within the program, such as a twenty-use-only facility.
- **Freeware** This can be distributed and used freely without any charge. The copyright of the software usually remains with the originator, but you can use it without having to pay. This type of software often consists of small utility programs and can also be found on web sites and cover discs.
- **Music** Computers today can download, play and burn music files on to CDs. Music is also under copyright. There have been cases of illegal copying and selling of music files. One web site doing this was closed down.
- **Graphics** Images can be easily captured or scanned using computer technology. This information is also protected by copyright. If you use images you could be infringing copyright law if you don't seek permission from the sources. You should check whether you can use graphics without permission.
- **Data** There is a market for lists of personal details that can be used by direct marketing companies to mail shot people on the lists with offers and other information. This could be by snail mail or through your e-mail inbox. All data is protected.

Remember:

The information contained on many web sites may also be protected by copyright – you need to check to make sure before you use any.

→ Check your knowledge

1. What are the four security zones in Internet Explorer?
2. What type of web sites might you put into your Restricted zones?
3. If you set a High security level, what protection will it offer?
4. What are cookies?
5. Why might you install a Firewall?
6. What should you look for when buying things online?
7. What function would you use in Internet Explorer to stop sites containing obscene language being loaded by your browser?
8. Why might a digital ID be useful?
9. What are the rules to follow when deciding on passwords?
10. What types of work are protected by the copyright laws?

Practice assignments

Practice assignment 1

This assignment is broken down into 4 parts:

1. A brief scenario is provided for candidates.
2. Task A requires candidates to locate information about Internet Service Providers using search tools and the Internet.
3. Task B requires candidates to locate information on virus protection using search tools and the Internet.
4. Task C requires candidates to send an e-mail with attachments.

You must, at all times, observe all relevant health and safety precautions.

Time allowed: 3 hours

Scenario
You work for Bin 13 Office Supplies, a small company that operates a mail order office supplies business. They are interested in using the Internet to communicate with their suppliers and customers. James Leung, the Senior Manager of the company, has asked you to research the best ISP for the purpose. As he is concerned about security on the Internet following some fairly hair-raising stories in the news recently, he also wants you to find out about virus protection and other ways of ensuring security of communication over the Internet.

Task A

1. Read the information in the scenario.
2. Load your browser software and connect to the Internet.
3. Use suitable search tools to find Internet Service Providers. Identify *three* different ISPs and note the web addresses.
4. Visit your *three* web sites and find the following information and note this down:
   (a) The name and URL of each of the ISPs.
   (b) Amount of web space offered.
   (c) Support service offered.
   (d) Number of e-mail addresses offered.
   (e) Whether it has a local access number.
   (f) Subscription charges (£ sterling).
5. Open your word processor and enter this information. Save it with the filename ISP.
6. Using the History information, reload each ISP's homepage and add it to your Favorites or Bookmarks folder. Take a screen print of your Favorites folder and label it FAVORITES. Print out a copy.

7 Create a new folder in your Favorites and call it ISP. Move the URLs of the ISPs into this folder. Take a screen print of your Favorites folder and label it FAVORITES 2. Print out a copy.

8 Close down browser software and disconnect from the Internet.

Task B

1 Load your browser software and connect to the Internet.

2 Identify suitable search tools to use to find web sites that offer virus protection software. Use *three* different search tools and note down the web addresses:

(a) a directory search tool
(b) a meta search tool
(c) a keyword search engine.

3 Use each of your search tools to identify *one* appropriate virus protection web site and note these down.

4 Visit your *three* web sites and decide which is the most appropriate for the needs of the company. Using this site, find out the information about the protection offered by this software and the cost.

5 Save this information as VIRUS and print out *one* copy.

6 Add this URL to your Favorites folder.

7 Using the History feature, reload *one* of your search tools and find a site which provides information about viruses which are currently in circulation.

8 Copy the relevant text from this web page into a new word processing document. Save this file as CURRENT VIRUSES.

9 Reload your virus protection software site from your Favorites folder and check to see if it will provide protection against the current viruses. Take a screen print of the appropriate page and label it VIRUSES IN CIRCULATION. Print out a copy.

10 Close down browser software and disconnect from the Internet.

Task C

1 Use an e-mail software package to write a message containing the information James has requested and send it to him at his e-mail address (which will be supplied by your tutor). You should include the following information:

(a) That a file is attached containing information about possible ISPs.
(b) That a file is attached containing information about an appropriate anti-virus software package.
(c) Details about *one* security measure you can take using the settings in Internet Explorer to protect against viruses.
(d) Details about *one* way a virus can be transmitted through the Internet and why this might be harmful.
(e) Details of *one* current virus in circulation.

2 Attach the files ISP and VIRUS to your e-mail.

3 Print out a copy of your e-mail.

4 Send a carbon copy of the e-mail to your tutor and a blind carbon copy to yourself.

5 Send the e-mail.

6 Check your Inbox for new messages and produce a screen print of your Inbox which shows that your Bcc has arrived. Label this INBOX and print out a copy.

7 Delete the Bcc from your Inbox and produce a screen print to demonstrate that this has been done. Label it DELETED and print out a copy.

8 Exit the e-mail software program and disconnect from the Internet.

Practice assignment 2

For this assignment you will need to have e-mails already sent to you. Ask your supervisor or tutor to prepare them for you.

The tutor will create e-mail 1 with text Document 1 as an attachment and e-mail 2 with text Document 2 as an attachment and send them to the candidate's e-mail box for them to access:

Document 1

"USES OF THE INTERNET

booking holidays
online banking
shopping from your own home
researching information
maps and route finding facilities
downloadable software
communication with friends and family over the world"

Document 2

"SAFETY ON THE INTERNET

(a) security of web sites
(b) unpleasant material
(c) viruses
(d) junk mail
(e) hackers"

This assignment is broken down into 4 parts:

1 A brief scenario is provided for candidates.

2 Task A requires candidates to open and save e-mail attachments.

3 Task B requires candidates to identify some of the security risks involved in using the Internet.

4 Task C requires candidates to send e-mails with attachments.

You must, at all times, observe all relevant health and safety precautions.

Time allowed: 3 hours

Scenario

You work for a firm of architects, Ali, Hird and Partners, who have two offices in Wales. As a Personal Assistant to the Senior Partner, Hanif Ali, you work in the main office producing reports, proposals and specification documents, as well as finding information about the use of IT to improve the firm's effectiveness. Hanif has asked you to do some research into the safety risks of increasing the firm's use of the services available on the Internet.

Task A

1 Read the information given in the scenario.
2 Load your e-mail program and connect to your Internet Service Provider.
3 Retrieve and read e-mail 1 that has been sent by the other partner in your firm, Monty Hird. Save the attachment to your shared area or hard drive (your tutor will tell you where to save your files).
4 Open the saved attachment in your word processing program and print out a copy.
5 Retrieve and read e-mail 2. Save the attachment to the appropriate area.
6 Open the saved attachment in your word processing program and print out a copy.
7 Produce a screen print of the two e-mails in your Inbox. Label it INBOX and print out a copy.
8 Produce a screen print of the two attachments saved to the appropriate area. Label this SAVED ATTACHMENTS and print out a copy.
9 Close down your e-mail program and disconnect from the Internet.

Task B

1 Open Document 1 in your word processing program and using the information in Document 2 indicate next to each of the different uses for the Internet which security risk from the list (a)–(e) might be applicable for each one. You may find more than one risk for each use.
2 Print out a copy of your document and save it with the filename RISKS.
3 Load your browser software and connect to the Internet.
4 Identify suitable search engines to find web sites that will provide information about security protection on the Internet. Find security prevention measures for *three* of the security risks highlighted in your document RISKS.
5 Note down the URLs of the search engines you used and the number of hits each search produced.
6 Add to your Favorites or Bookmarks folder the URLs of the web sites where you found the information needed.
7 Save the web pages containing the information you have found with the filenames SECURITY 1, SECURITY 2, SECURITY 3.
8 Create a new folder in your Favorites and name it SECURITY. Move the URLs you have bookmarked into the new folder.
9 Produce a screen print of your Favorites folder showing the URLs in the SECURITY folder you have created. Label this SECURITY and print out a copy.
10 Use the History feature to reload the information from the web page you saved as SECURITY 1 and print out a copy.
11 Close your browser and disconnect from the Internet.
12 Open your saved files SECURITY 2 and SECURITY 3 and print out copies.

Task C

1. Use an e-mail software package to reply to Monty Hird detailing the three safety risks you have identified and possible preventative measures which could be taken. Attach the files: SECURITY 1, SECURITY 2 SECURITY 3, for his information.
2. Send a carbon copy of the message to your tutor and a blind carbon copy to yourself.
3. Produce a screen print of your e-mail message showing the attachments and the recipients' names and e-mail addresses. Label it SECURITY E-MAIL and print out a copy.
4. Make the message high priority and send the e-mail.
5. Retrieve your Bcc and produce a screen print showing the Bcc in your Inbox. Label it INBOX 2 and print out a copy.
6. Delete the Bcc from your Inbox.
7. Close down your e-mail program and disconnect from the Internet.

Solutions

Section 1 Getting started

Check your knowledge

1. See **World Wide Web**, page 3.
2. See **Equipment for connecting to the Internet**, page 3.
3. **a** HTML (HyperText Markup Language). The text-based language used to write web pages.
   b ISP (Internet Service Provider). The ISP acts as a gateway to the Internet.
   c FTP (File Transfer Protocol). A set of protocols needed to copy files over the Internet.
   d Browser. A program that translates the information on the Net into documents that you can see on screen.
   e URL (Uniform Resource Locator). The unique address of a web page.
   f HTTP (HyperText Transfer Protocol). The standard set of rules governing how web pages are transferred over the Internet.
4. See **How fast can you go?**, page 4.
5. The domain name gives details about where the computer is located.
6. 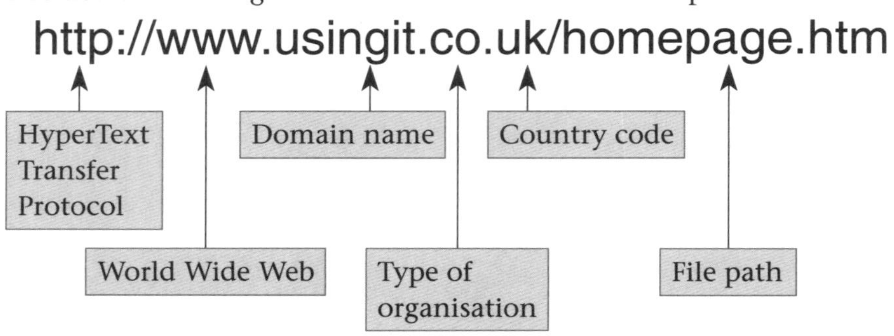

7. See **What's on the Internet – Communication**, page 8.
8. A way of doing business online.
9. See **Pros and Cons**, page 12.
10. See **Beware of Viruses**, page 13.

Section 2 Getting connected

Check your knowledge

1. See **Online Services and Internet Service Providers**, page 15.
2. See **Internet Service Providers**, page 16.
3. See **Choosing an ISP**, page 18.
4. You are only charged for your time connected at local charge rates.
5. If your computer is used by several members of the family.
6. Your own data.
7. Bits per second.
8. An account with ISP or Online Service.
9. To check the conditions of using the software.
10. Homepage can be the page the browser displays when it first starts or the first page of a web site.

Section 3 'Surfing' the Net

Check your knowledge

1 The mouse pointer will change to a hand with a pointing finger as you move it over a hyperlink.
2 The folder where you would save your favourite web site addresses.
3 The name for the Favorites folder in some browsers.
4 Enter the URL into the address box in your browser and press Enter.
5 Use the up or down arrow keys by the **Days to keep pages in History** box in the Internet Properties dialogue box.
6 Because of the risk of a virus being transmitted.
7 A search engine is an index of web pages. A directory has the data sorted into categories.
8 See **Searching**, page 48.
9 A meta search site submits the keywords entered to multiple search engines at the same time and produces one list of hits.
10 A printout of the whole web page will be produced.

Section 4 Keeping in touch

Check your knowledge

1

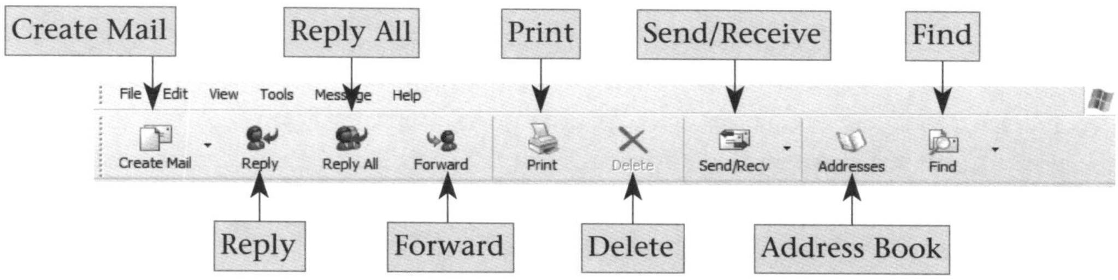

2 You can send and receive e-mail messages from anywhere in the world.
3 A computer, a modem, an e-mail program and an account with an Internet Service Provider.
4

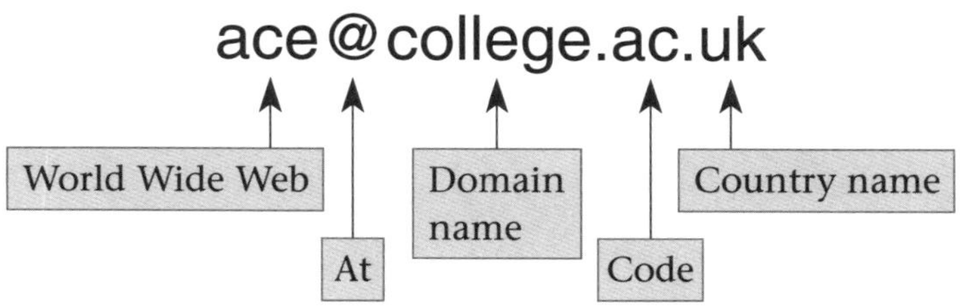

5 **a** The messages you have received
b The messages you have sent
c The messages you have deleted – or maybe nothing at all if you have emptied your Deleted Items folder!
6 Bcc: Blind Carbon Copy.
7 It's taken as shouting, according to Netiquette.
8 Unread messages are emboldened.
9 Examples could include: word processed documents, images, sound files, video files, computer programs.
10 To tidy the Inbox.

Section 5 Safe surfing

Check your knowledge

1. Internet zone, Local intranet zone, Trusted sites zone, Restricted sites zone.
2. Web sites that could potentially damage your computer or data.
3. You are unlikely to download a file containing a virus.
4. Small text files from web sites which can be stored on your computer.
5. A Firewall would be installed to prevent unauthorised access to a computer over a network.
6. Check the web site is secure by looking for a closed lock icon.
7. The Ratings settings in the Content Advisor.
8. A digital ID can prove your identity in electronic transactions. It can also be used to encrypt your messages.
9. See **Passwords**, page 95.
10. The work of an author or artist, including software programs.

Glossary

Attachment	A file which is sent along with an e-mail message.
Bookmark	Also called **Favorite** in Internet Explorer. A list of frequently visited, marked sites to enable one click access.
Browser	The program that allows you to view web pages on the Internet.
Bug	A faulty piece of coding in a computer program.
Cookies	Information stored as a text file on your computer from web sites you have visited.
Directories	Listing of web sites classified into subject areas.
Domain	Part of the name for an Internet computer that tells other computers where it is and the type of organisation that owns it.
Download	Obtaining a file from a web site usually by clicking on a word or icon on the page.
E-commerce	Buying and selling products and services online.
E-mail	Electronic mail. A way of sending messages from one computer to another across a network.
Encryption	Files that have been coded that can't be read without a special key.
Favorite	Also called **Bookmark**. A list of frequently visited, marked sites to enable one click access.
Freeware	Software that is free to use.
FTP	File Transfer Protocol. The system used to transfer files from one computer to another.
Hacker	Someone who gets unauthorised access to a computer to look at, change or destroy data.
History	A record of the URLs you have visited stored in a list by your browser.
Hit	A web page found by a search engine in response to keywords entered into a search box.
Homepage	The front page of a web site, or the opening page in your browser.
HTML	HyperText Markup Language. The language used to produce web pages.
HTTP	HyperText Transfer Protocol. The system used to transfer web pages over the Internet.
Hyperlink	Used to jump from one web page to another. Hyperlinks can be images or underlined text.
Internet	The network of interconnected computers that communicate using special protocols.
IP	Internet Protocol. The system used to specify how data is transferred over the Internet.

IP Address	The unique number which identifies each computer on the Internet.
ISDN	Integrated Services Digital Network. A high speed telephone connection which can transfer data over the Internet very quickly.
ISP	Internet Service Provider. Companies which provide a gateway to the Internet.
Keyword	A word that represents a document's contents.
Link	A connection between two computers. Highlighted text or images which connect web pages.
Mailbox	The place where e-mail is kept on an ISP server.
Netiquette	Informal rules about the way to behave on the Internet.
Network	Computers linked together to share information and services.
Offline	Not connected to the Internet.
Online	Connected to the Internet.
Online Services	Company that provides access to its own network as well as to the Internet.
Page	A document or information available on the Internet.
Plug-ins	Features added to the browser to give extra functionality, such as playing music, reading special text formats.
POP	Point of Presence. A point of access to the Internet.
Protocol	A set of rules used by computers to communicate with each other.
Search engines	An online service that will search web pages for keywords entered in the search box.
Shareware	Software which you can try before you buy.
Snail mail	Mail delivered by the normal postal system.
TCP/IP	The language computers on the Internet use to communicate with each other.
Upload	To copy a file from your computer to another computer via the Internet.
URL	Universal Resource Locator. The address given to all the different resources on the Internet.
Virus	A destructive program hidden in other files and programs that can damage files on your hard drive.
Web page	A document written in HTML and linked to other documents by hyperlinks. Shown as a single screen in your browser.
Web site	A collection of web pages set up by an organisation or individual.
World Wide Web	The friendly face of the Internet. Formatted text and graphics which make up pages on the Internet.